CHESS FOR BEGINNERS
A PICTURE GUIDE

Also published as
Picture Guide to Beginner's Chess

By
AL HOROWITZ
Three-Time U.S. Open Champion
Editor of CHESS REVIEW
Chess Columnist, NEW YORK TIMES

PERENNIAL LIBRARY

Harper & Row, Publishers
New York, Cambridge, Philadelphia, San Francisco
London, Mexico City, São Paulo, Singapore, Sydney

Published in 1959 by Barnes & Noble, Inc.
by special arrangement with Z. E. Harvey, Inc.

ISBN: 0-06-463223-7

Dedicated by the author to his wife Edna

87 88 89 90   20

Designed by FRANK ANGELINI
Printed and Bound in the U.S.A.

FOREWORD

The popularity of the game of chess is growing day by day. Literally, millions of chess sets have been sold in this country in the past ten years. A chess problem appearing in the New Yorker evoked 3300 replies. Nearly 25,000 books have been written on the subject in different languages.

These figures are astounding and they contradict the common notion that chess is a difficult game beyond the reach of ordinary intelligence. On the contrary, they signify a deep and abiding love which springs from intrinsic goodness.

We, in the States, have a proud chess heritage. Paul Morphy, New Orleans prodigy, was the first uncrowned chess champion of the world. Benjamin Franklin's *Morals of Chess* is an excellent dissertation on the virtues of this fascinating pastime. And we have produced great players and teams which have won the world championship on a number of occasions.

To meet the ever-increasing interest in this royal pastime, new techniques in teaching have been devised. A hundred years ago all kinds of fanciful verbiage described a simple movement. Today, a short, simple, clear, understandable code defines the same action. Today, photographs give the learner the feeling that he is actually handling the chessmen as he is learning. All of the latest techniques are employed here to appeal to youngsters and oldsters alike.

This book is dedicated to the new generation of chess-players. May they uphold our proud heritage.

Al Horowitz

TABLE OF CONTENTS

FOREWORD iii

THE ORIGINAL SET-UP 1
   The Board 1
   The King and Queen 3
   The Bishop 3
   The Rooks 3
   The Knights 4
   The Pawns 4

THE MOVEMENTS OF THE MEN 6
   The Rook 6
   The Bishop 7
   The Queen 8
   The King 11
   The Knight 12
   The Pawn 13
   Pawn Promotion 15
   En Passant 17

THE KING IS IN CHECK 20
   Out of Check 21
   Check By A Knight 22
   Double Check 22
   Illegal King Move 23

CHECKMATE 24
   Examples 25

CASTLING 29
   You May Castle 29
   You May Not Castle 29

STALEMATE 32
   Examples 32

UNDER-PROMOTION 36
   Examples 36

RECORDING A CHESS GAME 38
    Notation 38
    The Files 39
    The Ranks 40

PLAY YOUR FIRST GAME 42
    Illustrated Game No. 1......................... 42

MORE ON CHESS NOTATION 57

SCORE SHEET 60

A BIT OF PLANNING 61

A TRAP 61

THE GAME IS A DRAW 63
    Rules and Regulations 63

RULES OF FORMAL PLAY 70
    The Time Clock 71

COMPARATIVE VALUES 72
    The Rule of Thumb 72

MATERIAL IS IMPORTANT 79
    Gain and Loss 79
    Noah's Ark Trap 81
    Double Attack 84

KNOW YOUR ENDINGS 87
    Elementary Mates 88
    Elementary Endings 92

HINTS FOR THE OPENING 107
    General Principles 107
    An Actual Game 111

LESSONS IN STRATEGY AND TACTICS Illustrated 115
    Illustrated Game No. 2 116
    Illustrated Game No. 3 124

THE ORIGINAL SET-UP

A chess game is a battle.
The chessboard is the battlefield.

As you see, a chessboard is composed of eight rows of eight squares each — a total of 64 squares. These are alternately light and dark. Regardless of their actual color, the light squares are referred to as the white squares. The dark ones are called the black squares.

A chessboard must be placed so that each of the two players has a white square in the right-hand corner.

The chessmen are the armies.

Some are white and some are dark. The light-colored chessmen are called the white pieces. The dark ones are the black pieces.

The player with the white pieces is referred to as White. The player who has the black ones is referred to as Black.

Except for color, the two armies are identical. Each has six varieties of chessmen.

In a standard set, they look substantially like this.

| King | Queen | Rook | Bishop | Knight | Pawn |

Below each piece, you have not only its name, but the symbol that is used to represent it in chess-diagrams.

Each of the armies contains 1 King, 1 Queen, 2 Rooks, 2 Bishops, 2 Knights, 8 Pawns. That is, each has 16 men.

Each player has his army marshalled on his own side of the chessboard. They line up in the last two rows nearest to himself.

Notice how the two groups of 16 men line up in identical fashion.

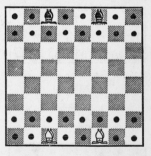

The King and Queen, the two most important pieces, stand in the middle of their forces. Each King faces the opposing King, each Queen the opposing Queen. The white Queen is on a white square and the black Queen on a black.

Each of the royal figures has a Bishop in attendance.

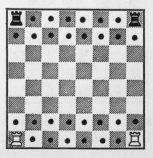

A Rook is placed in each corner of the chessboard.

The Knight stands between the Bishop and the Rook. The back row of pieces may be likened to the officers.

A row of Pawns, like a rank of simple soldiers, stands in front of these officers.

As the battle starts, the chessboard looks like this. Before you begin your game, check that your pieces are right. Also check for the mistakes that appear below and on the next page.

WRONG   RIGHT

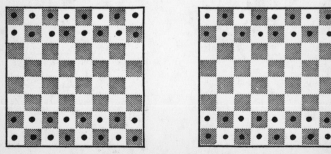

Look at the color of the square in your right-hand corner. It should be white — not black.

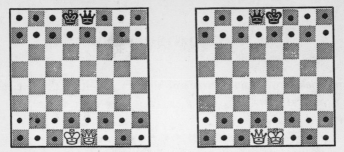

WRONG   RIGHT

The White Queen stands on a white square, the Black Queen on a black square.

Each of the six types of chessmen moves in a different way. Each has its special powers. And, to balance this, each has certain limitations.

This interplay of powers gives the game of chess its peculiar fascination. The diverse elements combine to form almost numberless patterns. What is more, each of these patterns is not merely vivid and colorful. It is alive with a competitive excitement.

If you do not know the rules and look at a game in progress, it seems very confusing. Some of the pieces may go forward. Others, backward, sideways and obliquely. Some pieces may move one square. Others may go two or three, or even the whole length of the board. From time to time, one of the pieces is removed.

You may think this difficult, but these seemingly haphazard moves are all made in accordance with a number of simple rules. In the following pages, we will describe and also illustrate these rules.

The brief time it will take to learn them will be a small price to pay for the many years of pleasure that the game of chess can bring you.

THE MOVEMENTS OF THE MEN

The Rook moves any number of squares on either the horizontal or the vertical rows.

In this picture, the Rook has a choice of four directions. These are indicated by arrows. The Rook can stop in any of the squares which these arrows traverse.

We will have occasion to use such words as rank, file or diagonal.

A *rank* is a horizontal row of squares. (In the diagram, R-R.)

A *file* is a vertical row of squares. (In the diagram, F-F.)

A Rook moves along the ranks and the files.

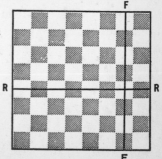

A diagonal is a series of squares — all of which are the same color — running in an oblique direction.

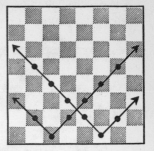

The ranks may be described as running East and West. The files go North and South. The diagonals run NE, NW, SE and SW.

There are 13 white-colored diagonals and 13 black ones.

The Bishop moves any number of squares on either side of its diagonals.

In this picture, the Bishop has a choice of four directions. These are indicated by arrows. It can stop in any square which these arrows traverse.

Because of the way it moves, a Bishop that starts the game on a white-colored square has to stay on a White square. A Bishop that starts on a Black square has to stay on a Black square.

In the original position (see p. 3), each side has one Bishop on a White square and one Bishop on a Black square.

The Queen combines the powers of the Rook and the Bishop. It moves any number of squares on its rank, its file or its diagonals.

In this picture, the Queen has a choice of eight directions. These are indicated by arrows. It can stop in any square which these arrows traverse.

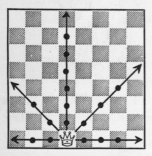

Thus, it has a choice of 27 different moves. Its path may be obstructed by its own or enemy pieces. But, if the path is clear, it never has a choice of fewer than 21 moves. (See diagram.)

The Queen is by far the most powerful piece on the chessboard.

You may wonder how a Queen got to be a powerful warrior. Though the game of chess is ancient, this is not a reference to the Amazons. The real reason is as follows:

Chess came to Europe from the Middle East where this piece was called a *firz*, that is, a vizier or counselor. In Europe, this became a *ferz* or *fers*. (That is what the Queen is called in Chaucer's *Book of the Dutchesse*.) Then, because the sounds were similar, the French began to call it a *vierge* — or virgin — a term which implied the Virgin, Our Lady, Queen of Heaven.

In Russia, it is still a *ferz*. In France and Germany, it is still a *dame* or lady. Since it stands beside the *King*, there are many countries (including England and America) where this piece is a *Queen*.

The Queen, the Rook and the Bishop are long-range pieces. If they please, they move only one square. But they also have the power of moving as many squares as they like in the particular direction they are going.

This is only true, however, if their path is not obstructed. As a rule, their way is blocked by either friendly or enemy pieces. Except when making capture, a piece cannot move to a square that is occupied. It can move only to a square that is vacant.

A Queen, a Rook or a Bishop does not have the power to move *beyond* any occupied square.

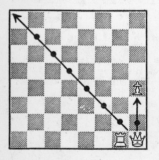

A player lacks the right of capturing his own pieces. (Only enemy pieces can be captured.)

In this diagram — the White Queen cannot move on the rank. It is blocked by the White Rook.

It can move 2 squares on the file. After that, the White Queen is blocked by the White Pawn.

The diagonal is not obstructed. The Queen can therefore move to any square on the diagonal.

Only enemy pieces can be captured.

The Queen, the Rook or the Bishop can capture any enemy piece that is in its moving-range. (The Rook captures on the ranks and files, the Bishop on the diagonals. The Queen captures on all three of them.) It removes the captured piece and goes to the square on which the captured piece was standing.

In this diagram, the Rook can capture the Black Pawn. It cannot take the White Pawn.

The Rook takes the Black Pawn. The Black Pawn is removed. The Rook goes to the square where the Black Pawn was standing.

The White Queen can capture any of the 8 black chessmen that are obstructing it.

The White Bishop cannot take the Black Knight. (The White Rook is in the way.) The White Bishop cannot take the Black Pawn. (The Black Bishop is in the way.) The White Bishop can take the Black Bishop. On a subsequent move, it can capture the Black Pawn.

In checkers, you have to capture any time that you can. In chess, a *capture is optional*. There may be a number of reasons why another move would be preferable. In the diagram to the right, the White Queen can capture the Black Bishop. This, however, is inadvisable.

Can you see the reason why?

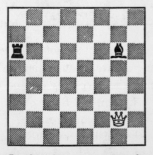

In this diagram, notice the location of the Black Rook.

The White Queen has captured the Black Bishop. But the White Queen, in its turn, can be taken by the Black Rook.

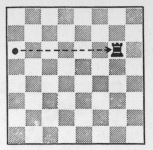

The Black Rook has captured the White Queen. The White side has lost the Queen. It has captured a Black Bishop. Since the Queen has more power than the Bishop, the White side has lost in the transaction.

The King moves — *one* square at a time — on the rank, the file or the diagonal. He captures in the same way that he moves. He can take any enemy piece that is on an adjoining square.

In this picture, the King can move to any square that is marked by a circle. He can take an enemy piece standing on any one of these squares.

As you have noticed, the King moves in the same directions as the Queen does. But, having a limited range, the King is less powerful. The King, nevertheless, is *the most important* chessman. (On p. 18, you will see the reason why.)

In this picture, the Knight can move to any of the squares that is marked by a circle. It can take any enemy piece that is standing on one of these squares.

When thinking of the Knight-move, there are two things to remember. (a) The Knight moves *2 squares* away from its original position. (b) The Knight moves to a square that is of the *opposite color*. Note that, in the photograph, the Knight is standing on a white-colored square. It has 8 possible moves. Every single one of these moves takes it to a *black-colored square*.

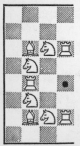

The Knight's move is a cross between those of the Bishop and Rook. It moves 2 squares. One of these is on the diagonal, the other on the rank or file.

If it helps you to visualize it, you can think of the Knight's move as being something like an 'L.' Or — like a fish-hook.

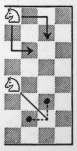

The Knight is the *only piece that has the power to jump over other chess-pieces*. When a Knight is capturing — or when moving to an empty square — it is not blocked by units that are on the intervening squares. It does not matter whether these pieces are enemy or friendly. The Knight — or horseman — is able to leap over them.

The White Knight, in this diagram, can capture the Black Bishop even though there are Black pieces intervening. The Knight can also move to the square marked by a circle.

It can capture the Black Bishop though White pieces are intervening. It can also move to the square that is marked by a circle.

Note that, in each diagram, the Knight moves to a square that is of the opposite color.

The Pawn moves *forward* on the file. The Pawn is the only chessman that lacks the power to move backward.

On its initial move, a Pawn has the choice of moving either *one* or *two* squares. In this picture, the Pawn may move to either of the squares that is marked by a circle.

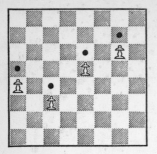

On any move after its first one, a Pawn moves *only one square*.

The Pawn has more special rules than any of the other chessmen. For example, a Pawn is the only piece that does not capture in the same way that it moves.

It moves vertically — on the file. It captures on the *diagonal*. The Pawn can capture any enemy piece that is *one* square diagonally *in front of it*.

In this picture, the White Pawn can capture the Black Rook. It cannot capture the Black Pawn or the White Knight. Neither can the Black Pawn take the White one.

A Pawn is blocked by any piece that stands in front of it.

On its next move, the Pawn will come to the end of the chessboard. When it does so, there will be no place to go forward. And, as we have seen, a Pawn is the only piece that lacks the power to move backward.

Unless there were a special rule to take care of such a situation, this Pawn would have to stay there as a sort of permanent obstruction.

There *is* such a special rule. When it reaches the end of the board, the Pawn gets *promoted*. The Ugly Duckling turns into a Swan. Or, in Army terms, the soldier becomes an officer. The Pawn becomes a different piece. And — just as in the Army — this process is known as *promotion*.

A Pawn can't become a King. But it can be transformed into any of the other pieces: a Knight, a Rook, a Bishop — or even a Queen. (As Napoleon said: Every soldier carries in his knapsack the baton of a Marshal.)

It stands to reason that a player will probably select the most powerful piece on the board as a new addition to his army. He will usually choose a Queen.

This is known as *queening the pawn*.

It does not matter how many Queens a player has at the time. A player — theoretically — can *queen* every one of his Pawns, and have 9 different Queens at one time. In actual practice, it is rare, however, for a player to have more than 2.

Since a chess set has only a single Queen, his second Queen creates a problem. It is usually solved by using an inverted Rook. There are occasions (see p. 36) when another piece is preferable. A player may choose a Rook, or a Bishop or a Knight.

This is known as *under-promotion*.

The earliest surviving records dealing with the game of chess are found in India. They date back to about 500 A. D. They are written in Sanskrit.

At that time, chess was clearly a military game. The Knight was a horseman; the Pawn, a foot-soldier. That is what they are today. But, as opposed to this, the Bishop and the Rook were different. The Bishop was an elephant; the Rook, a chariot.

In these records, chess is called *chaturanga* or *four arms*. Because of this, it has been thought by some that chess originally was a four-handed game. In this interpretation, the *four arms* are four armies. It is more probable, however, that this name refers to the four arms — the four branches of the service: Pawns, Bishops, Knights and Rooks . . . Foot (infantry), elephants, horsemen and chariots.

The King and Queen — that is, the King and Vizier — stood in the middle of these troops. Like their modern counterparts, the elephants stood beside them. The more mobile mounted soldiers, on horses and in chariots, were located in the wings. The foot-soldiers stood in front of them.

In those days, the game was slower. The Rook and Knight had the same moves that they have at present. The Bishop and the Queen, however, had much less power. The Pawn could move only 1 square —even on its first move.

Then the game was speeded up. The new Pawn-move led to earlier action. The extra power given to the Bishop and the Queen led to a greater tension. But, at first, these reforms, although exciting, went a little bit too far. For one thing, the Queen at one time was given the additional powers of the Knight. Experience showed that such power was excessive and the Knight-move was withdrawn. In addition, it developed that the 2-square Pawn-move had one undesirable consequence. The purpose of this move was to create a position that was tense. But there was one situation where this Pawn-move made for dullness. In the first position, there were po-

tentialities of many exciting maneuvers that were based upon a Pawn-move. In the second diagram, White has moved his Pawn 2 squares and, by doing so, he has locked the position.

In order to take care of this situation, there is a special rule. White can still make this Pawn-move. But, if he does so, his opponent has the privilege of capturing *en passant*.

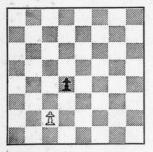

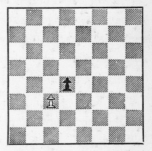

In this diagram, the White Pawn has the choice of moving either one or two squares.

If the White Pawn moves one square, the Black Pawn can capture it.

If the White Pawn moves up *two* squares, it does not evade this capture. The White Pawn may be taken in exactly the same fashion as if it had moved only *one* square.

This is called capturing *en passant*.

The White Pawn is removed. The Black Pawn *does not take its place.* It moves one square on the diagonal (as if the White Pawn had moved one square.).

A player may capture *en passant* immediately. If he fails to do so, he forfeits the privilege.

Both sides try to win the battle. In chess, this is done by capturing the enemy King.

As you will see, the King is never actually taken. When a player is certain to lose his King on the very next move, the game is *automatically over*. That player *loses*.

A player may resign his game even though his King is not immediately threatened. But, even then, he does this because he sees that, no matter what he may do, the King will eventually be captured.

It is the fate of the King that decides who wins the battle.

Thus, the King — though it is far from being the most powerful piece on the chessboard — is decidedly the most important. In a similar fashion, Charlemagne is not as mighty as either Roland or Oliver; King Arthur is a weaker fighter than Sir Tristram or Sir Lancelot.

Yet these monarchs are the most important members of their armies. If they were killed or captured, the whole battle would be lost. Because of this, their soldiers make every effort to protect them. At the same time, they try to assail the enemy King. In the course of the battle, they fight with the enemy soldiers, but this is only secondary. They fight with these other soldiers because, if they kill enough of them, they will have superior forces and, in that way, find it easier to accomplish their objectives: 1) defending their own King; 2) attacking the enemy's.

The following diagrams illustrate positions in chess where the King is threatened with capture. In these circumstances, the King is said to be *in check*. The term *check* is more clearly defined in the next chapter.

In this diagram, the Queen is checking the Black King on the diagonal. The Queen may also check on the rank and the file.

Here the King is not in check. But, if the White Knight moves, the White Queen will check the King. This is known as a *discovered check*.

Black is not in check. But, if the White Pawn takes the Black one, *both* the White Pawn and the Queen will be checking the Black King.

This is called a *double check*.

The player who is threatening to capture the enemy King has to warn his opponent that his King is in danger. He does this by announcing "Check!"

THE KING IS IN CHECK

When a chessman threatens to take the enemy King on the next move, it is *checking* the King. The threatened King is *in check*.

Any piece — except the King — is able to check the enemy King.

In this diagram, the Rook is threatening to capture the King. The Black King is in check.

Here it is the White Knight that threatens the Black King. The King is in check.

In these diagrams, the Bishop and the Pawn, respectively, are checking the Black King.

When a player sees — and hears — that his King is in check, he *must* make a move which will take the King *out of check*.

Any other move is illegal.

If there were no such rule, the following situation might arise.

In this diagram, the White Bishop is threatening to capture the King. The King must move out of check!

Let us now suppose, however, that instead of doing this, the Black player moves his Pawn.

If such a move were legal, the Bishop would capture the Black King. Thereupon — the game would be over.

But — the Black player might say that White did not say "Check!" *That* is why he did not notice that his King was attacked. Then, the White player might insist that he actually *did* say "Check!" The whole thing might result in a very unpleasant situation. To make such quarrels impossible, this regulation was made:

A player cannot stay in check *if he can possibly get out of it.*

There are three different ways in which a King may get out of check.

1 By having the King move to a square on which he no longer ·is in check.
2 By capturing the checking piece.
3 By placing a piece between the checking piece and the King.

The Rook is checking the Black King on the file. If the King moved on the file, he would still be in check.

To get out of check, the Black King steps away from the line of attack.
He could have moved to any of the other squares that are marked by a circle.

The Black King is checked by the White Bishop. Either the King or Rook can capture this Bishop. When the Bishop is off the board, the King ceases to be in check.

The White Queen is checking the King. Either the Black Rook or the Black Bishop may be interposed between the White Queen and the King. If either one of them does so — then the Black King is out of check.

The Knight is attacking the Black King. Since the Knight is able to leap over any intervening pieces, it will be useless for the Black Rook to interpose.

It is not possible to interpose on a Knight check.

It is also impossible to interpose on a double check. In this diagram, the Rook can move between the White Bishop and the King. The Queen, however, still would be checking the King. Likewise — the Black Bishop could move between the White Queen and the King. But, if it did, the King would still be in check because of the White Bishop.

As a rule, if a player wants to make a weak or a foolish move, that is his privilege. There is no way you can stop him. This is true, of course, in every sphere of activity. In the game of chess, however, there is one type of blunder which has been declared illegal.

A player *cannot* make a move which exposes his King to an immediate capture.

Thus —as we have seen — a player cannot stay in check. The other cases are similar.

The King cannot move into check.

The King cannot take a piece if that piece is protected by one of the enemy chessmen. (This would be equivalent to his moving into check.)

A player can't move any piece if that piece stands between his King and *immediate* capture.

The Black King cannot move to the square that is marked by a circle. Since this square is on the White Queen's diagonal, such a move would be moving into check.

If a White man were on this square, the Black King could not capture it. That move would expose the King to *immediate* recapture.

The Black Knight cannot move. If it did, the White Rook would capture the King.

In this diagram, the Rook is *pinning* the Knight.

The Knight is *pinned*.

CHECKMATE

If the King is in check and, no matter what he does, he cannot get out of check, then his side has lost the game.   The King is *check-mated*.

A typical *mate* (or *checkmate*) is shown in this photograph.

The King is in check.   The Queen is threatening the King on the short diagonal.

The King cannot get out of check.   There are three possible ways (see p. 21) in which a player may get out of check.   In this position none of these is available.

The King cannot move out of check.   If the King moves on the diagonal, he will be taken by the Knight.   If he moves horizontally, he will be captured by the Queen.   Thus, either King-move is illegal.   (Notice that the King is blocked by the presence of his own Rook.   If the Black Rook were not there, that would be an escape-square.)

The checking piece cannot be captured.   If the King captures the Queen, he will be taken by the Knight.   Thus, this capture is illegal.

No Black piece can be interposed between the checking piece and the King.

This being the case — *The Black King is checkmated.*

The White side has won the game: and Black has lost it!

It is easier to force a checkmate if, as in the following diagrams, the hostile King is standing on a rank or on a file that is at the edge of the chessboard. (It is the easiest when the King is near a corner.) Then the King has fewer escape-squares!

In this position, a single piece (the Rook) is enough to cause a checkmate. The Black Rook could not do this if the White King were not blocked by the presence of his own Pawns.

Here two pieces force a checkmate. The White Queen does most of the work. It not only checks the King, but will take him if he moves on the file or the diagonal. The Knight stops the only loophole — a King-move on the rank.

The White Rook and the Knight combine to mate the King. The White Knight has a dual function. It protects the checking Rook and it stops the King from moving on the file.

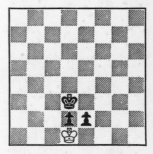

Though a King cannot give a check himself — (do you see the reason why?) — it can be of aid in effecting a checkmate. The Black King, in this diagram, not only protects the Pawns. It stops escape on the diagonal.

The important thing is checkmate. It does not matter if a player has weaker — or fewer — pieces than his opponent. He will win if he is able to checkmate the opposing King.

Since this is so, a player has no qualms about sacrificing even his most powerful units in order to achieve a mate. In this sequence of diagrams, we will see how Black loses his Queen, yet, despite this, wins the game.

In this position, Black can force a pretty mate.

Black checks the King. The latter cannot take the Queen because it is protected by the Knight. White has no choice.

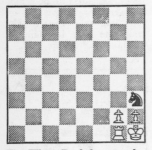

The White Rook has to take the Queen.

This sacrifice of the Queen brings the Rook to block the King. Now the Black Knight checks — and Checkmate!

For obvious reasons, this is called a *smothered mate*.

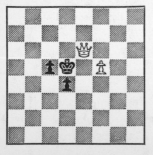

A mate is also possible in the middle of the chessboard. The King cannot take the Queen because the White Pawn protects. The King has 5 other moves — but, in every case, the White Queen controls those squares.

Notice that the King is blocked by the 2 Black Pawns.

The White Queen is checking the Black King on the rank. The Black Knight cannot interpose. If it did, the White Bishop would capture the King. The Black Bishop cannot interpose either. If it did so, the Black King would be taken by the Rook.

The Black Bishop and the Black Knight are *pinned*.

The Knight is checking the King. Black's black-square Bishop is covering the one escape-square. The White Pawn cannot take the Knight. It is pinned by the Black Rook. The White Rook cannot take the Knight. It is pinned by the other Bishop.

The result is checkmate.

In this case of double-check, Black is able to handle either one of the checking pieces, but Black is checkmated because he **cannot** handle both of them. As for the Queen check, Black is able to interpose any of 4 different pieces, but this won't answer the Knight-check. Two pieces can take the Knight (the Black Queen and the Pawn). But this won't answer the Queen check.

Here is an interesting checkmate.   Note that, to achieve it, White has sacrificed his Queen. The moves that lead to this position will be given and discussed on pp. 42 to 56.

Since this position is complex, the relevant parts of the checkmate are shown in this diagram.

Do you see why this is mate?   (See p. 56.)

CASTLING

Each of the players tries to checkmate the opposing King. While doing so, he tries to stop the similar attempts of his opponent. He must always be concerned with defense as well as offense.

If a player wishes to move his King to a place where he is safer, he is sometimes able to use a maneuver known as *castling*.

This involves the King and either one of his Rooks. In this maneuver, *both* pieces travel at *one time*: but it *counts as only one move*. (There is no other occasion when a chess-player can move two different pieces at one time.) The term *castling* is suggested by the Rook, which is sometimes referred to as the Castle.

If the King and Rook are in their original positions —

If neither of these pieces has previously made a move —

If the squares between them are not occupied —

Then, subject to certain restrictions — (these are discussed on the following page) — the King and the Rook may move in the fashion shown in this picture.

It is not legal to castle into a check. In this diagram, the King would be subject to capture by the enemy Bishop.

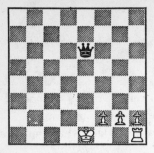

Castling is not legal when the King is in check. If the player gets out of check without moving his King — i.e., by capture or by interposing — this player retains the right of castling later.

It is not permissible to castle over a check. Here the King would have to pass a square that is covered by the Black Rook.

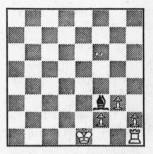

This is legal. A Rook can castle even when this Rook is threatened by an enemy piece (in this case, the Bishop).

We have seen how the King castles when the Rook is on the King's side. In this photograph, he castles on the farther side, the Queen's side.

Note that, in each case, the King moves *two* squares when castling. (This is the only occasion when a King moves more than one square.) But where, on the King's side, the Rook moves 2 squares, here — being farther — the Rook moves 3 squares.

When one castles *long* — that is, on the Queen's side — one situation arises which cannot come up on the King's side. In this diagram, the Rook is going to traverse a square, (this square is marked by a circle), on which it is subject to capture.

In this position, however, it is legal to castle.

The other regulations are similar to those for castling on the King's side.

The principal purpose of castling is to ensure the safety of the King, by removing him in one move nearer a corner of the board and away from the direct fire in the center. Another purpose is to permit better cooperation of the forces.

STALEMATE

A player who is losing his game sometimes has one last resource. He may get a *draw by stalemate*.

In this position, the White player is on move. The White King is in check. White has no legal moves. (No matter where he goes, his King is subject to capture.) White is *checkmated*.

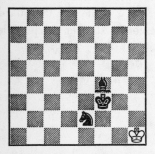

In this position, White is also on move, but the White King is *not* in check. White has no legal moves. (No matter where he goes, his King is subject to capture.) White is *stalemated*.

When a player is *not* in *check* and he has *no legal moves* — that game is *drawn*.

The player is stalemated.

White on move. The King has no legal move. A Knight and a Pawn alone are not enough to cause a checkmate. But, in this position, they suffice to cause a stalemate.

The Black King has no legal moves. The Queen is the only piece that can stalemate, single-handed.

The Black King is stalemated. Black has a Pawn, but it has no moves either.

The White King has no legal moves. There are two White Pawns, but both of them are pinned. It's a stalemate!

This rule may seem arbitrary, but, by and large, it makes a more exciting contest.

In this position, White has a very simple win — but he goes about it carelessly.

The White Queen checks. It would have been better to go to the square marked by the circle. Nonetheless, White still has an exceedingly easy win.

Black has made the only legal move. Now, if White is careless, the Black King will be stalemated.

White is careless. The King-move has removed the Black King's only legal move. The White Queen should have moved to the square marked by a circle. Mate in 2 moves would have followed!

Here, because he was absent-minded, the White player was penalized. Instead of a certain win, he has no better than a draw. No experienced player would ever make this error. Yet the principle would still apply. Even at the highest levels, fear of stalemate keeps a player on the alert.

In the previous set of diagrams, the Black player was passive. When White got careless, Black got the benefit of stalemate. He himself, however, had nothing to do with getting it. In the following situation, Black takes a positive step by which he actually earns the stalemate.

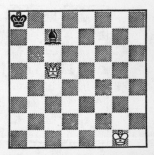

Black on move. White has the superior position. A Queen against a Bishop is normally enough to win. But, in this specific case, Black still has a resource.

Black threatens the White Queen. The Queen is pinned. It cannot get off the diagonal. Thus, it has no choice.

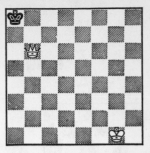

White takes the Bishop. Now the Black King is stalemated.

You may have wondered why a player who had the chance to make his Pawn a Queen would sometimes choose to make it a Rook, a Bishop or a Knight. The fear of a stalemate is most frequently the cause for such an *under-promotion*.

In this diagram, Black — who is on move — has a chance to Queen his Pawn.

If he does, the White King is stalemated.

If he makes the Pawn a Rook, the White King has a move. The game is not a stalemate: and, as we shall see, a Rook is enough for eventual victory.

UNDER-PROMOTION

There is one other reason for under-promotion. On certain rare occasions, a Pawn becomes a Knight. It thus gets an important *check* which it could not get otherwise. By this check it disrupts the plans of the opponent.

In this position, the White Pawn can take the Rook. When it does, it has the option of becoming a Queen.

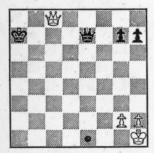

But, if it Queens, the *Black Queen* will move to the square that is marked by a circle. The White King will be *checkmated*.

Instead of this, the White Pawn becomes a Knight. It does this with a check. The Black King must get out of check. Then, when it does, the White Knight *takes the Queen*. After this, White wins at leisure!

On p. 37, you will see how White was able to create this situation.

The White player deserves credit for this clever under-promotion. But, before this, he did something even finer. He *envisaged* the position a couple of moves earlier. Then, he made it happen.

White seemingly has the worst of it. The Black Rook is threatening mate. The Black Queen is also threatening the Pawn.

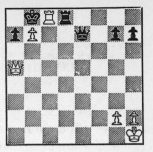

In his seeming trouble, White takes an aggressive measure. *The White Rook checks!*

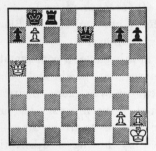

The Black Rook takes the White one. (If, instead of this, the Black King takes the Pawn, the White Rook takes the Black one!)

The White Queen now captures the Black Pawn and checks. Black's best move is for him to take the Queen. (Do you see the reason why?)

By his dazzling series of moves White has set up the stage for the winning under-promotion.

It is always good to see.   It is *better* to foresee!

Recording a chess game

We have been looking at many photographs and diagrams. For that matter, we will do so in the future. It is an accepted fact that such graphic aids are useful for the purpose of instruction.

Actually, they are helpful not only to beginners. Since a picture takes the place of a large number of words, one will come across many diagrams even in a book for experts. But, on the other hand, there are also times when visual aids are cumbersome.

Take a game of 40 moves (that is, 40 for *each player*). Each move would require 2 diagrams: one for White and one for Black. Thus, a game of 40 moves would call for 80 diagrams.

That is not all. At different points in this game, a commentator would wish to tell you *why* certain moves were made and others weren't. These explanations would require even more diagrams. All in all, there might be several hundred for each game. At such a rate, it would take no more than 4 or 5 games to fill up an entire volume! These difficulties are solved by having a descriptive notation — a sort of *chess short-hand*. This notation can be used without any diagrams at all — but the best results are obtained if one judiciously blends both of the alternative methods.

A chess notation, in order to be effective, has to have a code of symbols for each piece and for each square.

The symbol for each piece is, in general, the *first letter* of its name.

K = King
Q = Queen
R = Rook
B = Bishop
P = Pawn

In the case of the Knight, the initial is not enough. Like the King, it also begins with a *K*. To differentiate it from the other, an additional letter is needed. Because of this, *Kt* has traditionally been the symbol for the Knight. But, the Kt (Knight) is sometimes still confused with the K. So, in recent years, it has increasingly become the practice to use an N for the Knight. Thus this piece has *two* entirely different symbols.

N or Kt = Knight

In this book, we will always use N to stand for the Knight.

Each player has 2 Rooks. The symbol R is not enough to tell us which of his Rooks is involved. (This is also true of his 2 Bishops and 2 Knights.)

The answer is in this diagram:

Queen's Side   King's Side

Queen's Side   King's Side

The chessboard may be divided into a King's side and a Queen's side. Each King's side has a Rook, a Bishop and a Knight. The Queen's side has a similar complement. Thus, each player has both a King-Rook and a Queen-Rook or, in terms of symbols, a *KR* and a *QR*. He also has these pieces: KB, KN, QB, QN, or — to spell it out — *King-Bishop, King-Knight, Queen-Bishop, Queen-Knight.*

Q R	Q N	Q B	Q	K	K B	K N	K R

Names of Files

Let us also notice that, in the original position, each of the White pieces stands on the identical file as the corresponding Black piece. We can therefore name the files according to these pieces. A file has the name of *that piece which is on it in the original position.*

Each Pawn has the name of the file in which it is standing, KRP, KNP, etc. When a Pawn makes a capture, it moves to a different file. Then it takes the name of *that* file!

Each file has a single name. Each rank has *2* names.

The rank nearest to each player is his *first*. The next one is the *second* rank. So on . . . . until the *eighth* rank. But what is nearest to one player is, necessarily, farthest from the other. Each of the players therefore has his own system of counting.

In this diagram, the names (numbers) of the White ranks are given on the right, of Black ranks on the left. The numbers of each rank always give a total of 9.

Numbers of Ranks

Each square is an intersection of a rank and a file. In order to locate a square, we must give its rank and file. (In effect — its latitude and its longitude!) In this diagram, the square is on the Queen-Bishop file. It is White's Queen-Bishop Three. It is Black's Queen-Bishop Six. Or, in terms of chess notation, it is White's *QB3*. It is Black's *QB6*.

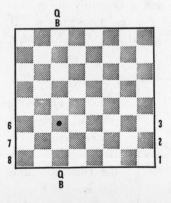

When White is moving, we count ranks from the *White* side. When Black is on move we count from the *Black* side.

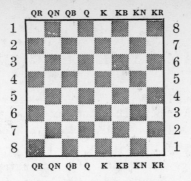

Here we have the names of the files and the alternate names of the ranks. To find the name of any square, intersect the file and rank.

– means *goes to*	For example, Q–Q2	The Queen *goes to* Q2.
x means *captures*	QxQ	The Queen *takes* the opposing Queen.

0–0	=	castles King-side
0–0–0	=	castles Queen-side
ch	=	check
dis. ch	=	discovered check
dbl. ch	=	double check
e.p.	=	*en passant*

Play your first game

In the following pages, we will show a sample game. All the moves will be transcribed. Then, for every move, we will also show a photograph. Usually we will show a move on one page and its picture on the next one. In this way, if you wish, you may be able to test your knowledge of notation. After you have figured out what each move is going to look like, you can check it with its photograph.

This is the *starting position.*

Sometimes, there are games with handicaps. To make the fight more even, a stronger player may remove one or even more of his pieces. But, unless otherwise stated, it is always taken for granted that each game is going to begin with the units set up as above.

In this position, the King, Queen, Bishops and Rooks cannot possibly make a move. Nevertheless, the first player has the choice of *20* different moves. Each Pawn moves 1 or 2 squares. (The 8 Pawns have 16 moves.) Then, each Knight has 2 moves (to R3 or to B3).

It is a law of chess that *White always makes the first move*.

In.this sample game, White moves *P–K4*.

1 P–K4

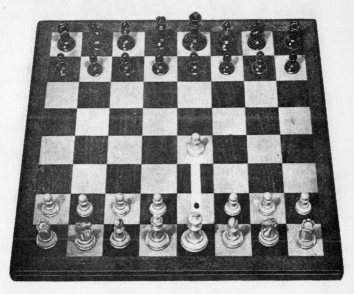

The King-Pawn moves from King 2 to King 4.

It is not necessary to say *KP–K4*. Since no other Pawn can go to that particular square, P–K4 is sufficient.

In this picture, the White Pawn is on King 4. King 2 is marked by a circle. (In this sequence of photographs, the square from which a move starts will be designated in this fashion.)

This move opens diagonals for the Queen and King-Bishop. *White now has a mobility which he did not have before*.

This is the traditional way of beginning a chess game. Nowadays, an expert is more likely to play such moves as P–Q4 ·or P–QB4. But, for a beginner, P–K4 is advisable.

He will *learn most* while playing it.

Black responds with *P–K4*.

1 . . .   P–K4

Like his opponent, Black had 20 moves at his disposal: but he chose to play what White did. And this move brought him similar advantages.

Experience has shown that other moves are also satisfactory (such moves as P–K3, P–QB4, N–KB3, P–QB3). Yet, for a player who is learning, P–K4 is advisable.

The players make *alternate moves*. In certain games, a player need not take his turn (for example, the Japanese game of *Go*). In chess, however, a move is compulsory. If White makes a first move, Black unless he chooses to resign must also make a first move.

Note the way the move is written.

1 . . .   P–K4

The dots after the number indicate that this is Black's move. White moves *N–KB3*.

2 N–KB3

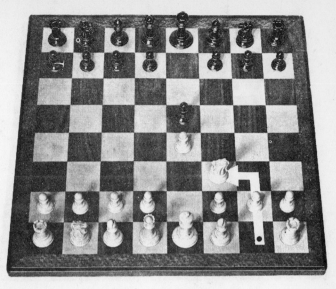

White moves Knight to King-Bishop 3.

It is not necessary to say *KN*–KB3. Since the other Knight can't go to this particular square, N–KB3 suffices.

Before he made this move, the White player had the choice of *29* different moves. (Do you see that many?) Though not all of these were good, this shows that great variety which is one of the game's assets.

By his last move, White is *developing* this Knight. That is, White is getting his King-Knight into action. It is threatening to capture the Black King-Pawn. If White wished to move this Knight, he also had the choice of KR3 or K2. But neither one of these moves would have threatened the Black King-Pawn. Knight at King 2, in addition, would have blocked the Queen and Bishop.

Black moves *N–QB3*.

2 . . .   N–QB3

Black's Queen-Knight moves to Queen-Bishop 3. This both *develops the Knight* and *defends the Black King-Pawn.*

Black could have defended his Pawn in a number of other ways. But a move like B–Q3 — (check this on the photograph) — would have blocked the Queen-Pawn. Q–K2 would have cut off the King-Bishop. (The choice of opening-moves is like a problem in traffic!)

N–QB3, the move Black actually made, is the most usual response and, very possibly, the best one.

White plays *B–B4.*

3 B–B4

White moves his King-Bishop to Queen-Bishop 4. Since, in this particular position, his Queen-Bishop is blocked, B–B4 identifies White's move sufficiently.

Besides developing the Bishop, this move *clears the way* for *castling.*

Since White has the *first move,* he is in a better position to be the attacker. In the early part of the game, White has the *initiative.* For his part, Black defends himself. *But he keeps looking for chances to mount an offensive of his own.*

3 B–K2 would have been much too passive.

B–B4 is *aggressive.* It puts pressure on the Pawn at Black's King-Bishop 2. At the present time, the King defends this adequately. At some later point, however, White's pressure may be increased. Black may then find it difficult to defend it properly.

A threat need not be immediate; if one *builds up* an attack, that is equally aggressive!

Black moves *P–Q3.*

3 . . .   P–Q3

Black moves Pawn to Queen 3.

This move has two advantages. 1) It opens the diagonal for the Black Queen-Bishop. 2) It gives additional defense to the King-Pawn. The Black Queen-Knight, hitherto, had been its only protection. If that piece moved, Black would have lost his KP. Now the Knight is free.

This move also has a drawback. It blocks the KB diagonal. The only square at present available to the Bishop is K2. It might have been advisable for Black to do what White did and move his Bishop to B4 before he moved his Queen Pawn.

White moves *N–B3*.

4 N–B3

White's Queen-Knight goes to Queen-Bishop 3. Since White's other Knight is already at King-Bishop 3, it is not necessary to say N–*QB*3. N–*B*3 identifies this move sufficiently.

White simply develops his pieces. Or, in military terms, he is *mobilizing his forces.* (For a player who is learning, this is by far the best plan.)

Other moves would have also served this purpose. For example, P–Q3, O–O or P–Q4.

Black now plays *B–N5.*

4 . . .   B–N5

The Black Queen-Bishop moves to King-Knight 5. It is **not** necessary, this time, to say B–KN5. In this particular **position,** B–N5 is sufficient.

By *pinning* White's King-Knight, this move *seemingly* stops it from moving. Black is also threatening to put extra **pressure** on this Knight by playing his own Knight to Queen 5.

The White player sees this — and he has *a plan of his own.*

White's move is *O–O.*

5 0–0

The White player castles.

The King-Knight still is pinned by the Black Bishop.

White could have broken this pin by moving B–K2. This, however, would have meant that his earlier move, B–B4, had been useless. (That is, he would have taken *2* moves to get his Bishop to King 2. He could have done this in *1* move.)

Black can now move N–Q5!

(Do you see what this threatens?)

If Black does this — *what does White have in mind?*

Black *does* move *N–Q5.*

5 . . .   N–Q5

Black moves Knight to Queen 5.

This move puts added pressure on White's Knight at KB3.

As a general rule, it is better not to move *one* piece *twice* in the opening. It is preferable to develop *two* different pieces. But, in this particular case, Black believes that he is going to get a specific advantage by his move of N–Q5.

The immediate threat is 6 . . . NxN ch. If 7 PxN, Black plays B–R6. This move threatens the White Rook which is now on KB1. (It is thought to be advantageous to obtain a Rook for your Bishop.) If it moves away to K square – Black plays Q–N4 ch. White's King must move R1. After which, Black plays Q–N7 *checkmate!*

How is White going to meet this? Is he forced to swallow his pride and retreat the Bishop to K2?

But — as we told you — *White has some plans of his own.*

White plays *NxP.*

6 NxP

White's King-Knight takes the King-Pawn.

Since the White Queen-Knight is not able to capture any Black Pawn, it is not necessary to specify that the Knight is the *King*-Knight. Since the King-Knight is not able to take any other Black Pawn, it is not necessary to say that this Pawn is the *King* Pawn.

Thus, in this particular position, NxP is sufficient.

Black relied too much on this King-Knight's being pinned. Seemingly — it could not move. If it did, White lost his Queen! But, in spite of this, White has blithely moved his Knight.

Has White overlooked this? Has he made a costly error?

Black plays *BxQ*.

6 . . .   BxQ

Black plays Bishop takes Queen.

When your opponent makes what looks like an obvious error, always take some extra time to make sure this isn't a *trap!* The 'error' may have been the bait that got you to fall for it.

In this particular case, Black too easily assumes that White has simply made a mistake.

As a matter of fact, instead of his taking the Queen, 6 . . . PxN was preferable. White would then play QxB. Black would then play NxP (the Pawn at White's QB2). After this, the game would be very far from over.

White plays *BxP ch.*

7 BxP ch

White's King-Bishop captures the Black King-Bishop Pawn, checking the Black King on the diagonal.

Do you see what is going to happen?
Black has only one move.
He must play it . . . *K–K2.*

7 . . .   K–K2

Black plays King to King 2.

The King could not go to Q2. Neither could it take the Bishop. The White Knight that is placed on K5 is what makes these moves impossible.

If Black had played his King-Bishop at some earlier point in this game, KB1 would have given the Black King an excellent escape-square.

As it is, the only possible legal move is 7 . . . K–K2.

White plays *N–Q5 checkmate!*

8　N–Q5 checkmate

White's Queen-Knight goes to Q5. Since the other White Knight could not, at this time, go to Q5, it is not necessary to write *QN–Q5*. N–Q5 is sufficient.

We have now reached a position that we have previously shown. Three White pieces have combined to make this checkmate. The Knight at Q5 checks the King. It also stops the King from going to Black's King-Bishop 3. The Knight at K5 protects the White Bishop. It also stops the King from escaping at his Q2. The White Bishop (at KB7) stops the Black King from going to either K1 or K3. The Black King is *checkmated!*

MORE ON CHESS NOTATION

Chess notation tends to be as brief as possible. As you may have noticed, it tends to go in for short-cuts. Thus, in the following diagrams, we will have *four* examples of a King-Bishop taking a King-Bishop Pawn. Yet, in only one of them, will we get the notation of KBxKBP.

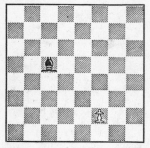

Here there are no other Bishops and there are no other Pawns. This is scored as BxP. (Incidentally, do you see why this is the King Bishop? Check in the original position. Black's King Bishop is on a black-colored square.)

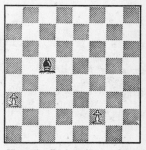

Here the Bishop has a choice of 2 different Pawns. It is therefore Bx*BP*.

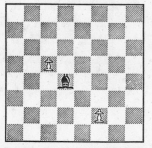

In this diagram, Bishop can take 2 different Bishop Pawns. To give the necessary information, one must say Bx*KB*P.

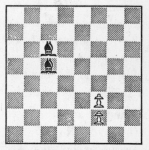

Here both of the Bishops can capture a King-Bishop Pawn. In that case, one must say *K*BxKBP.

One can also set up positions for KBxP or KBxBP.

Of course, in every one of these instances, the full notation

KBxKBP is *also correct*. But, in general practice, you will find that chess-writers use an economical notation, and you ought to be prepared for it.

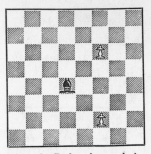

In this position, BxP means that the *King*-Bishop does the capturing. If the *Queen*-Bishop took the Pawn, the notation would have to be *BxP ch*. Notice, too, that White's QBP is *pinned*. Since this Pawn cannot move, P–B4 would mean that King-Bishop Pawn is the one that does the moving.

Here the Bishop has a choice of 2 King-Bishop Pawns. Since these Pawns are on White's KB2 and KB6 respectively, this would be recorded — depending on which Pawn he takes — as BxP (7) or BxP (3), from Black's side, since it is Black's move.

Here is another use for the parentheses. One cannot always keep track of which Rook is the King-Rook and which is the Queen-Rook. (Because each is on a different color, one can always tell about the Bishop. But one often has the identical trouble with the Knights.)

In this position, either Rook can go to Q2. For the one on B2, one would say R(2)–Q2. For the other, R(3)–Q2.

Parentheses are also used to indicate a Pawn-promotion. E.g., P–N8(Q) or P–B8(N).

The game we looked at went as follows:

White	Black	White	Black
1 P–K4	P–K4	5 O–O	N–Q5
2 N–KB3	N–QB3	6 NxP	BxQ
3 B–B4	P–Q3	7 BxPch	K–K2
4 N–B3	B–N5	8 N–Q5 mate	

In pictorial form, this 8-move game required all of 16 illustrations. Here it took less than one inch of type.

If you look in books, however — even in those chess-books that are plainly meant for experts — you will see a lot of pictures. If this game, for instance, happened to be printed in a chess-book, there probably would be a diagram after 6 NxP. In effect, this position is a major cross-roads. The game takes one decisive turn where it could have taken another. The editor discussing this game would mention the various possibilities, and he would give you this diagram so that you could refer back to it. Thus, you would get something like this:

6 NxP

6 . . . .   BxQ

Then, before he made the 7th move, the editor would suggest that, in the diagrammed position, 6 . . . PxN would have been much preferable. Then the editor might suggest how the game might go on from that point. (If 6 . . . PxN 7 QxB, NxP. These are known as *if-moves*.)

The editor might also like to give his *opinion* of a move. If he does, he has the choice of these symbols:

> !   that is a good move
> !!   a *very* good move
> ?   the move is poor
> ??   the move is TERRIBLE

In this game, he probably would write

6 . . . .   BxQ ??

Once you know chess notation, you will find that this new knowl-edge has numerous employments.   You can use it, for example, in order to record your own games.

Records tend to make things solemn.   We do not, as a general thing, recommend your keeping them.   You may have a rivalry, however, with one of your fellow-players.   You may play a match against him.   Or you may join a club and play in one of its tour-naments.   On such occasions — you may want to have things formal.

Also, you may want to play a friend in a different town.   If you know notation, you can play by mail.   (This is known as Cor-respondence Chess.)   A move and its answer ought to take you about a week.

You will also need notation if you want to follow the games that are currently being played by leading chess-masters.   One is seldom able to attend one of the important tournaments.   But, within a day or two, the scores of the more exciting games will be printed in some newspaper.   Later, these and other games will be printed in a magazine.   You can play them and enjoy them at your leisure. It is also likely that, before the year is over, there will be a book containing all the games of this tournament.

You are likewise able to enjoy the best chess games of the past. There are books of previous matches and tournaments.   Other books deal with the games of some famous chess-player, for example, those of Morphy.   On p. 111, you will find one of his brilliant per-formances.   Or, if you want thrilling games no matter what their source is, there are various anthologies.   One of the best of these is *The Golden Treasury of Chess.*

TYPICAL
RECORD
OF GAME

SCORE SHEET

DATE *November 15, 1956*   OPENING *Ruy Lopez*
WHITE *John Doe*   BLACK *Richard Roe*

	WHITE	BLACK		WHITE	BLACK
1	P-K4	P-K4	31		
2	N-KB3	N-QB3	32		
3	B-N5	P-QR3	33		
4	B-R4	N-B3	34		
5	O-O	B-K2	35		
6			36		
7			37		
8			38		

A BIT ON PLANNING

Let us go back to that game (pp. 42 to 56) which ended in an 8-move checkmate.

This game points up several morals.

First of all, you should remember that you have an alive opponent. If you are trying to beat him — *he* is trying to do the same to you.

You must *pay attention to his plans*.

Why did he make his last move? What is he planning to do next?

Being human — he is fallible. He will make his share of errors. When he does, you should exploit them. (That is how *most games* are *won*.) Yet you must never forget that he is trying to beat you! If he seems to make an error, this may be a part of his plan. It may actually be a trap that *he* has laid for *you*.

In this particular game, it was White, the winning player, who took the other into account. He anticipated that, on his fifth move, Black might play N–Q5. He prepared an answer to this move! As opposed to this, Black completely ignored the fact that his opponent had a mind and a purpose of his own. When — on his sixth move — Black saw he could take a Queen, he did not look. He simply leaped! As you saw, the consequences were disastrous.

When he made this error (6 . . . BxQ), White was ready to exploit it. The game was over in 2 moves!

In general, White won this game because he showed better judgment — because he had more prudence, more foresight and precision.

In more specific chess-terms, White won because his pieces were much *better developed*.

When White moved his Knights or played Bishop to Queen-Bishop 4, White did not, it is true, envisage this specific checkmate. He was putting his pieces in squares where they had a maximum potential.

He was not able to foresee when and how his chance would come.
Certainly, he could not tell that Black was going to make that error
which he did make.   Yet, when he got his chance, all of these pieces
were poised — ready for decisive action.

The Black units were not ready!

White, having the first move, had a natural lead in development.
Black allowed White to increase this.   He moved only *two* of his
pieces, the Queen-Bishop and Queen-Knight.

Turn to the final position.

If Black had moved his King-Bishop or played KN–KB3 — (both
moves are plausible) — there would not have been any checkmate.
Instead of doing this, Black moved his Queen-Knight *twice*.   He left
his King-side untouched!

In itself, this was not fatal.   On his 6th move, if he had played
PxN, his game would still have been playable.   But, when he did
make a mistake — he was not able to recover!

All of his pieces were in the wrong place.

Thus, the opening moves are more than merely preparatory.
They can *determine the whole game*.

On p. 107, we will again consider the very important questions
of opening-play and development.

THE GAME IS A DRAW

We are almost ready to look at a chess game as a whole.

The last two pages were in the nature of a preview. In them, we began to see how a game is won or lost. We intend to deal with this question more fully. But, before we do so, let us look at those chess laws and regulations that have not as yet been mentioned.

The most important of these are the laws concerning draws. One wins a game either when his opponent is mated or when the opponent resigns. By the same token, one loses a game when he resigns or is mated himself.

There is one more way in which a game may be ended. No one wins: no one loses. The game is a *draw*.

There are several ways in which a draw may be reached. Thus far, we have seen only one of these — the stalemate. The others are:

1. *Draw by Mutual Consent.*

The players feel that, since further play would lead to nothing but a draw, they might as well save their energy and call the game a draw immediately.

This decision may be influenced by the caliber of one's opponent. An attempt to win a game frequently requires taking chances. What is safe with one opponent may be fatal if it is tried with a player of higher quality. There are times when both players have so much mutual respect that they agree to stop their game after 12-15 moves. This is ironically known as a *grandmaster draw*.

That is not to say that it is bad to call a draw *by mutual consent*. One sometimes reaches a position where one knows that one can counter any threat by the opponent and that the latter can counter any threat. At such times, it may be best to stop the game and start a new one.

It is advisable, however, for a player who is a beginner to *play* his *games through to the end*.

He will learn more by doing so.

2. *Draw because of Inadequate Forces.*

Neither player has enough material with which to mate.

The simplest case is when both are down to their Kings. In this diagram, Black has the White King in the corner. That is ideal for checkmate. Yet the Black King cannot get any nearer to the White one without himself being subject to capture. But — such a move is illegal. Since the two Kings have to stay at arms' length from each other, this is necessarily a draw.

Neither are King and Knight enough with which to mate the other King. This is the closest that they can come to doing so. The White King, attacked by the Knight, has 3 possible escape-squares, N1, N2 and R2. There is no way in which the Black King is able to cover *all* 3 of them. In this diagram, he does not cover R2. This game is a draw.

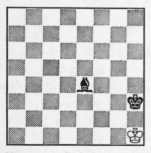

King and Bishop are not enough to effect a checkmate either. This is their best chance. The White King, in check, has 2 possible escape-squares, R2 and N1. The Black King is not able to cover both of them. **In this diagram, he has failed to cover N1.**

Note that, if you move the Black Bishop a square to the left, the White King is in stalemate. However, that is also a draw!

In this position, the White Knight at Bishop 6 is checking the Black King. If the Black King went to R1, the other White Knight would check at either B7 or N6. That would be a checkmate. But — there is no reason why the King should go to R1. If he went to B1, White — though he had 2 Knights — could not effect a checkmate. Barring a bad error by Black, this game has to be a draw.

In the first 3 diagrams, no matter how weak or ignorant the player with the lone King was, his opponent *could not* win. He had *inadequate forces*. In the last diagram (the one with the *two* Knights), White could not checkmate his opponent unless the Black player had an uncontrollable impulse towards suicide. To all effects and purposes, this was also a case of having inadequate material.

There are many positions which are in this last category. A knowledge of many of these is a necessary part of every player's equipment. We will look at these in the section devoted to *endgames* (pp. 87-106).

3. *Draw by Fifty-Move Law.*

In one of these drawn positions, a player may not realize that his chance for victory is zero. He may want to go on playing even though the other knows that such activity is fruitless. It is plain that this could go on forever.

In such cases, his opponent can invoke the *fifty-move law.*

This requires that, *in the next fifty moves,* the other player must either mate or show some tangible proof that he has made headway! If he cannot do so — it's a *draw.*

Tangible proof of progress is (a) making a capture, (b) moving a Pawn or (c) forcing a Pawn-move on the part of one's opponent.

The fifty-move rule is seldom used in games between experienced players.

4. *Draw by Repetition.*

If, in any game, the same position is reached *3 times,* then that game is a draw.

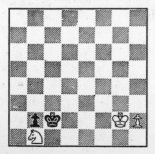

In this position, the White player is on move. He must stop the Pawn from Queening. If he does not — he will lose. On the other hand, if he can exchange his Knight for the Black Pawn, he will actually win.

N-R3 ch. If he makes any other move, Black's King will capture the Knight. If he does so, Black will win.

K-N6 — threatening the Knight. On any other move, White would win. He would simply go ahead with Queening his Pawn.

N-N1. Once again, White would lose if he made any other move. Depending on White's move, Black would either capture the Knight or Queen his Pawn.

N-N1 saves the Knight. It also blocks the Pawn. White is now threatening to Queen his own Pawn.

Black moves K-B7   (just as in the first diagram!): White moves N-R3 ch: Black moves K-N6: etc., etc.

Though each player has numerous moves, if either makes any moves except the one he does make, he will lose his game. This being the case, both keep repeating their moves. The third time they arrive at any one of these positions, either player may point this out and claim the game is a draw. (It is not a draw unless such a claim is made!)

It also happens that a player with a better game may not know what method he should use. He may stall till he gets a good idea or he may keep altering his plans. For either reason, he may carelessly permit a repetition of position and be very much surprised when his alert opponent points this out and claims a draw. (To prove that this has happened, he may have to show it on the score.

That is one of the reasons why in a serious game, players always keep a record.)

Note: it is not the *same* position if a *different* player is on move. *The same player has to be on move.* Otherwise — it's a different position!

5. *Draw by Perpetual Check.*

In some positions, one of the players is able to check his opponent indefinitely. If his game is otherwise inferior, he will take advantage of this and use this series of checks as a method of getting a draw.

Here Black will checkmate White the moment White stops checking him. Knowing this, White will not give him the chance. His Queen, shuttling between K8 and R5, keeps on checking the Black King. Since he can continue these two checks *ad infinitum*, the result is a *draw*.

In this diagram, Black has a choice of ways in which to move out of check. But, no matter which he takes, or no matter what he does on any of his subsequent moves, White can continue to check him. On any of these checks, Black can never interpose either his Pawn or his Queen. Because of this,

there is no way in which he can avoid a *perpetual check*. This game is a draw.

If Black refuses to admit this, White invokes the *fifty-move law*.

(In the previous diagram, White was able to invoke the rule on *repetition*.)

When a player gets a draw by means of *perpetual check,* it is frequently because of careless play by his opponent. In the last example, Black put his Queen into a square where it *was not in the game.* If, instead of this, Black had his Queen at Q6, he could quickly have put an end to the series of White checks.

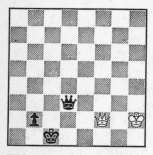

White's best move is to check at N1. Black interposes his Queen.

If White checks again, Black interposes once more — *and checks White on the rank.*

In other cases, however, a player must be ingenious. Thus:

In this position, if White checks at K8, Black moves *K-R2,* White cannot check at R5, because this square is controlled by the Black Queen at Q8!
As we saw on the previous page, Black is threatening *QxN checkmate.*

White moves *R-B1!* If QxR, the Black Queen has lost control of White's KR5. White has a *perpetual check.* If Black moves his threatened Queen, White exchanges Rooks and he has *at least a draw.*

A player with a winning game always has to be on guard lest his opponent find some ingenious way in which to force a *stalemate* or a *perpetual check.* If a player's King is exposed, he must be especially careful to prevent the latter from happening. In this connection, I remember an amusing end to a game I played against Pavey.

In this position, Pavey (Black) is on move. His game is greatly superior, and a player of his caliber should have no trouble winning it against any player in the world.

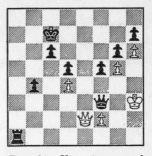

But his King is exposed. And Pavey feels that, as long as I have a Queen, I would have a chance to get *perpetual check.* (On my next move, for example, I may play Q-K7 ch.) So — he plays *QxBch.*

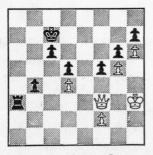

I have no choice. I must play *QxQ.* Pavey now plays *R-R6.* There's his subtle plan! My Queen is pinned. He'll exchange it for his Rook. With these pieces off, he will very easily win because he has more Pawns. No more fear of my getting *perpetual check.*

Black expects me to resign.

But, instead of doing this — I play *K-R4.*
Now, when he plays *RxQ,* my King has no moves. Instead of *perpetual check,* I have something just as good. I have a *stalemate.* Trying to avoid the frying-pan, he has fallen into the fire!

Rules of formal play

When you first begin to play, you may tend to be uncertain. You will start to move a piece . . . put it back . . . take another piece . . . change your mind . . . finger the first piece . . . etc., etc.

In a formal game, however, such fumbling is illegal. Once you touch a piece, you are compelled to move it. (This presumes, of course, that moving this piece is possible.) If you touch a hostile piece, you are compelled to take it.

If you want to touch a chessman only in order to adjust it, you should announce this fact *before you touch it*. The French phrase *j'adoube* is traditionally used for this action.

It may take you quite a while before you play a formal game — for example, a match or a tournament-game. But you need not wait for this. It is wise to use *touch-move* even in your off-hand play.

If you know that you cannot change your mind, you will get into the habit of *thinking before you move*.

It is also likely that, when you first play chess, you will tend to play slowly. This is understandable. But, as soon as you get to feel at home with the various moves of the chessmen, you should try to play more quickly.

There is a belief that a chess game takes forever. This is far from being the case. A chess game may be played at any speed that one chooses. In fact, in formal play, there is a pre-arranged *time-limit*. That is, a player must make a certain *number of moves* in a *stipulated time*.

This is a *time-clock*. It consists of two different clocks. These are so connected that only one of them runs at a time.

In this photograph, the clock on the left is running. (You can tell this by the lever.) The player on the left is *on move*. When he moves, he'll push the lever, whereupon his clock will stop. The other player's will start.

The time-clock runs only for the player on move.

A popular rate is *40 moves* in *2 hours*. A player takes as long as he likes for any one particular move. He can even take 1 hour and 59 minutes. But, if he does so, he must play the other 39 moves in the one minute that remains. (Here we have another reason for the players keeping score. They must know when they have completed 40 moves.)

The above rate averages out as about *3 minutes a move*. It would be good discipline to play your games at that speed. In fact, I would suggest that you play them even faster.

Do not hurry when your position calls for thought. But, on the average, take about a *minute a move*. This should enable you to have 3-4 games in one evening.

Comparative Values

As we have seen, the object of the game is to checkmate one's opponent. One can do this even if one has fewer pieces. But, on the whole, it is easier if one has more.

If all other things are equal, the gain of as little as a Pawn may be a decisive step towards an eventual mate. Though a player is prepared to give up any number of pieces any time his position calls for it, the more usual procedure is to attempt to get some advantage in material.

What constitutes such an advantage?

If one gains a piece for a Pawn and gives up nothing in return, that is clearly advantageous. But, as a usual thing, one has to pay some price. One gives up something in return. Since that is the case, as the game develops, one is often faced with problems. For instance, should one give a Rook up for a Knight? A Queen for two Rooks? A Knight for two Pawns?

To answer these, one has to know the relative value of the chessmen.

Every rule has its exceptions. A Pawn that is placed on a good strategic square may, at times, be more valuable than a Queen that isn't. By and large, however, the comparative value of the different pieces is as follows, in terms of Pawns:

Queen	9 Pawns
Rook	5 Pawns
Bishop	3 Pawns
Knight	3 Pawns

When exchanging pieces, keep the above table in mind. *Do not give up any material unless you have a good reason.*

(Since the King can't be exchanged, its value hasn't been given. In a sense, its value is infinite!)

To a large degree, the power of the long-range pieces is proportionate to their mobility. The more squares a piece can reach, the more things that piece can do: the greater is the likelihood that some of these squares are *good squares*.

Of course, their range is limited by their own or enemy pieces. For example, when the game starts, the Queen, Rook and Bishop do not have one move between them. In the case of the Rook, it will take it quite a while before it gets into action. Yet, in spite of this, one knows that, in the course of the game, they will get more elbow-room. Thus, at any point in the game, a player has to consider not only their immediate but their potential mobility.

If its path is clear, a Rook, no matter where it's placed, has a choice of 14 squares: 7 on the file, 7 on the rank. A Bishop that is posted on either K4, Q4, K5 or Q5 has a choice of 13 moves. As it approaches the sides of the board, the Bishop's range gets smaller. If it's posted on the 1st rank or the 8th rank or on either of the Rook-files, it has no more than 7 squares at its disposal. From this it follows that, depending on where it's posted, a Queen which is not obstructed has a range of 21-27 moves.

There are also other reasons why a Rook is better than a Bishop.

Thus, a Rook and King are enough to mate the enemy King. A Bishop and a King (see p. 64) are insufficient.

Since a Pawn moves on the file, a Rook is able to defend it during its entire progress. A Bishop cannot.

A Rook can keep a King out of the action. In this diagram, the Black Rook keeps the White King on the 1st rank. As the game progresses, such inhibitory action becomes increasingly important.

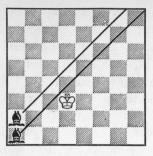

A lone Bishop is not able to shut out the enemy King. If the Bishop is on a White square, the King slips by on a Black square . . . It takes 2 Bishops to shut out a hostile King.

Two Rooks make a very effective combination. In fact, they are more than twice as powerful as one Rook. In this diagram, the two Rooks defend each other. If the Queen takes either one of them, the other will recapture. If they move along the rank they will *still protect each other*.

Since they stand on squares of different color, the two Bishops cannot do this. Notice, too, that the Rooks are threatening mate on either B8 or R8. This type of mate is frequently encountered.

Since they can get on a single rank or file, the two Rooks can concentrate on attacking a hostile chessman.

In this diagram, as in the other, they are threatening a mate. Thus, 1 . . . RxP ch 2 K–R1, RxP ch 3 K–N1, QR–N7 *checkmate*. (This is one of the common mating-motifs.)

When one lines up Rooks on the same file or rank, this is known as *doubling Rooks*.

Doubled Rooks are equally effective for purposes of *defense*.

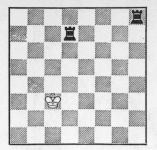

The two Rooks can mate without the help of other pieces. They can do this even when they are distant from the hostile King.

Here the two Black Rooks have a simple *mate in three*. (This phrase means that, no matter what White does, they will mate him in 3 moves.) Black moves R–B1 *check*. White must move to the Knight-file. Black moves R–N2 *check*. White must move to the Rook-file. No matter where he plays, R–R1 *check* is *checkmate*.

A Queen and Rook can cooperate in a similar fashion.

You may wonder why the value of a Knight is the same as that of a Bishop. A Knight that is posted in the corner has a choice of only 2 moves. (It can go to B2 or N3.) Its maximum range is 8 squares. As we have seen, a Bishop has a range of 7-13 moves. In addition, whereas a Bishop can move the entire length of the board, a Knight is able to move only 2 squares at one time. Not only this. It takes a Knight a number of moves to reach a square that is next to it.

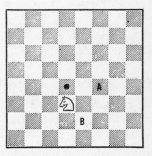

It takes a Knight 2 moves to reach the next square on the diagonal. In this diagram, the Knight must move to either of the squares marked *A* before it can go to the square marked by a circle.

It takes it 3 moves to reach the next square on the rank or file. Here it goes to A and B before it goes to the square that is marked by the black circle. There are other ways to reach it. But it can't be done in fewer than 3 moves.

It takes a Knight *2* moves to go 2 squares away on the rank or the file.

It takes it *4* moves to go 2 squares on the diagonal. This is not the only way — but no way can do this sooner.

This diagram shows how many moves it would take a Knight to reach all the points that are in a radius of 2 squares away from it.

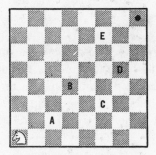

It would take a Knight 6 moves to go from one extremity of the long diagonal to the other. A Bishop could do it in *1* move.

Still a Knight, for all its slowness, can reach every square on the chessboard, whereas a Bishop is restricted to squares of a single color. A Knight, as we have seen, also has a special power. It can leap over its own and enemy pieces. So, although there are positions where a Bishop is superior, there are just as many cases where the Knight is clearly preferable. As you gain experience, you will learn to judge each case on its own particular merits. But, until you do, you may take it as a rule that a Bishop and a Knight are, in general, of equal strength.

Two Bishops, however, are usually stronger than either two Knights or one Bishop and one Knight.

In the case of Pawns, we have something else to consider. In itself, a Pawn is weak. Unless it captures, it cannot get off its file. It can't go backwards. And, except on its first move, it travels only 1 square at a time. Yet — it is potentially a Queen. And, as the game progresses and it gets nearer to *promotion,* it gets more and more value.

In the beginning of the game, a *minor piece* — (that is, a Bishop or a Knight) — is worth about 3 Pawns. On the other hand, if a Pawn is about to Queen, the other player will be willing to give up a Rook for it.

In the end-game, there are many positions in which a King and 2 Pawns beat a King and a minor piece or even a King and a Rook.

One occasionally has a chance to give several pieces for a Queen or, conversely, to give up the Queen for 2-3 pieces. It isn't always easy to decide if it pays to do this.

According to our table — (see p. 82) —

A Queen	=	9
A Rook and minor piece		
(Bishop or Knight)	=	8
3 minor pieces	=	9
2 Rooks	=	10

We can take this as a guide. Yet, in each position, we also have to consider whether or not these pieces coordinate. In general, if they do this, the Queen is inferior. If they do not do this, then the Queen is superior.

In these diagrams, we will look at two aspects of the Queen *vs.* 2 Rooks.

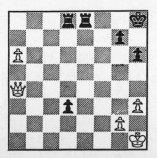

Here the Rooks cooperate. They defend each other. They control an important rank, as well as 2 strategically important files. White is on move; the White Pawn, like the Black one, is only 2 squares away from queening. Yet White is helpless.

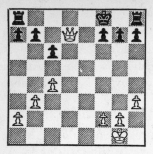

Here Black is on move, but cannot stop the Queen from capturing at least 2 Pawns. By that time, the Black Rooks will have managed to get together, yet the advantage of 2 Pawns ought to be decisive.

MATERIAL IS IMPORTANT

Since a Queen is stronger than a Rook, it is *stronger than both Rooks* as long as they are not organized and it can deal with them separately. (The advantage of having the Rooks together is one of the reasons for *castling*.)

One should notice, too, that in the early part of the game the Rook is fenced in by other pieces. It has little freedom of action. (This is true of all the chessmen, but especially of the Rook.) Thus, in this part of the game, the Queen is superior to *two* of them. As the game progresses, a Rook gets greater scope and becomes proportionately stronger. When they get together, the two Rooks, as a rule, get to be stronger than the Queen.

According to our table, 2 minor pieces (6 points) should be worth a Rook and 1 Pawn. There are many positions in which a player can exchange a Bishop and Knight for a Rook and a Pawn. In general, he should not do this. In actual practice, 2 minor pieces are worth a Rook and 2 Pawns.

The question of a Rook *vs.* a Bishop or a Knight is one that arises frequently. Here the answer is quite simple. A Rook is almost always stronger than either a Bishop or a Knight.

To get a Rook for either of these pieces is known as *winning the exchange*. If one does so, one is an *exchange ahead*.

As the table would indicate, a Rook is worth a minor piece and 2 Pawns.

Try to gain material. But, when doing so, be sure that the material *plus* does not entail a *positional minus*.

When, of your own free will, you choose to *give up material*, you should be doubly sure that your calculations are sound and the position that you get is more than worth this sacrifice.

There are several ways in which a player may gain material.

The other player can *make a mistake*. He may play a unit to a square where it is subject to capture. (When a piece is subject to capture, it is said to be *en prise*.) Or — he may not notice that a unit is attacked. Consequently, he may not move it or defend it.

Another form of oversight is for a player to forget to give a piece an escape-square. When this piece is attacked, he has no way to save it.

Because of its position on the chess board, a Rook is frequently the victim of this kind of blunder. This is illustrated in these diagrams:

Another common example is where the Bishop gets cornered by a group of advancing Pawns.

Here White moves P–N4, attacking the Bishop. When the Bishop goes to N3, White moves P–B5.

The Black Bishop is trapped.

As you gain experience, you will get to recognize such situations. You will be less careless. Also, since you will be playing against better players, you will have less occasion to profit by your opponent's carelessness. Even then, this *motif* will continue to come up — though in a less apparent form.

An example of this is the so-called *Noah's Ark Trap*:

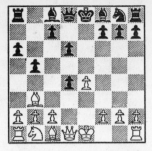

In this standard position, if White plays B–Q5, Black plays the Rook to N-square. After B–B6 ch , Black moves B–Q2. White plays BxB ch. Then, when Black recaptures, the White Queen takes the Pawn at Q4. The position is even.

Instead of this, White plays QxP at once. This is *an error.*
As in this diagram, Black moves P–QB4. This is followed by P–B5. The Bishop is trapped.

Beginners do not have a monopoly on blunders. The finest players in the world have been known to leave a Pawn or Queen *en prise.* They have even been known to overlook a mate on the move. As a rule, however, a good player's lapses take a more sophisticated form.

He is more likely to *miscalculate.* Thinking, as such players do, in terms of a sequence of moves, he occasionally overlooks something that is going to happen near the end of this sequence. Thus, an enterprising player will sometimes give up material, thinking it will bring him profit a number of moves later. There is a defense, however, that he has not anticipated. Because of this, the plan turns out to be unsound.

For example —

Visualizing this position, White gave up a minor piece all of 4 moves earlier. Black is on move. But, since the Knight is pinned, White will recover the piece — with a much superior game. (White threatens PxN ch, PxP; BxP ch, KxB; Q–R4 ch. White will actually win a Queen.)

Or so it seems. As a matter of fact, there is a defensive resource the White player has failed to see. Black plays Q–Q4. On PxN ch, Black plays PxP. The situation is reversed! Now the White Bishop is pinned. Black will have a marked advantage in material.

Up to this point, the examples have been rather passive. They have been based on the other player's errors. *He* has left a man *en prise*: *he* has made an unsound sacrifice. He has been the active agent.

When you first begin to play, if you gain material, it will be because of your opponent's errors. As your game improves, you will start to do things on your own initiative.

By taking positive action, you may force the other player to give up material in order to stave off a loss that is even more serious.

Here Black is threatening mate (the *smothered mate* shown on p. 26). The only way for White to stop this, is for the Rook to take the Knight.
Black wins the *exchange*.

The Black King has no escape-square. To provide it, he must move his Bishop to R3.
White wins the *Bishop*.

The only way to stop this mate is by interposing a Pawn. On P–K4, White plays BxP checkmate.

Black plays P–Q5. White plays BxP ch. Now, on P–K4, the Black Rook defends it.

White has gained a *Pawn*.

Here Black has managed to get his Pawn to the 7th rank. If White does not take it, Black will be able to Queen it.

White plays BxP ch.

Black has a *Bishop* for a *Pawn*.

In these examples, the gain of material was the by-product of an attempt to mate or — in the last case — to Queen. More frequently, one gains material by an attack which aims directly at its capture.

In general, such attacks fall into two different classes. In the first, one concentrates one's power against some enemy weak point. The latter is not able to meet this. The second is the *double attack*. One makes two threats at one time. On his next move, the other player is able to defend only against one of them.

White attacks the Pawn with 4 different units. Black defends with only 3. On 1 NxP, NxN; 2 BxN, BxB; 3 RxB, RxR; 4 QxR. After all that bloodshed, White has captured a Pawn.

White again attacks the Pawn with 4 different units. Black defends with 3. But, because the Queen and Rook are inverted, it does not pay White to make these multiple exchanges.

When making multiple exchanges, one should have one's minor pieces in front of the major. This applies to the defense as well as the offense. On 1 NxP, RxN; 2 BxR, QxB; 3 RxQ, BxR, Black does not lose a unit, but having lost a Queen, he loses material.

When a piece is pinned, it may easily become the target for a concentration of material. Pinning and attacking the Knight at either King or Queen Bishop 3 is **a very common motif.**

The simplest form of double attack is where a single piece attacks 2 different pieces.

The Black Knight threatens both the White Queen and Rook. White is able to move only 1 of them.

The White Rook checks and, simultaneously, threatens the Pawn. It would also win this Pawn, if the Rook and Pawn were inverted, or the Rook and the King.

Here the Bishop threatens both the Knight and the Pawn. It would also win this Pawn if the Bishop and Knight were inverted, or the Bishop and Pawn.

Even Pawns are capable of double threats. In this diagram, the Pawn attacks both the White Bishop and Knight.

The Queen, of course, is the piece *par excellence* for making a double attack.

After 1 P–K4, P–K4; 2 P–KB4, B–B4 — if White plays PxP, Black plays Q–R5 ch. It checks like a Bishop and attacks the KP like a Rook.

On P–N3, Black plays QxKP ch. Here the Queen checks like a Rook and attacks the Rook like a Bishop.

The Queen and Rook threaten the Pawn at White's QR7. Queen and Bishop attack the Pawn on White's KN7.

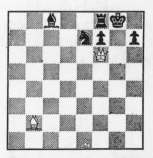

White's last move Q–B6 threatens mate on 2 different squares: KN7 and KR8. The Black Knight can stop either one of these threats. It cannot meet both of them.

If one has a *plus* in material, one is sometimes able to use it in order to force an early checkmate. However, this is not always feasible. What one does more often is to simplify the position. By exchanging pieces, the player brings it to a point where he has a winning end-game.

But before he can do this successfully, a player has to know when he *has* a winning end-game and when he *hasn't*. For example:

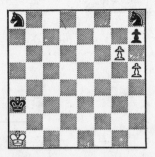

In this position, the Black player is on move. He must take the Pawn. (If he doesn't, White moves P–N7. Black cannot stop it from queening.)

Now there are two different ways in which Black can take this Pawn. On 1 PxP, PxP; 2 NxP — Black has gained a Pawn. He has a King and 2 Knights against a bare enemy King. But, as we have seen (on p. 64), this is merely a *draw*. If he knows this fact, Black does not play PxP.

On 1 NxP!, PxN; 2 PxP — Black has lost a Knight; yet he has a *winning end-game*. In fact, he does not need the other Knight on QR1. In this particular position, the Black King and Pawn are *sufficient material*.

KNOW YOUR ENDINGS

If a player knows his end-games, he will sometimes draw a game that he would otherwise lose.

In this position, White has a choice of taking either Bishop or Pawn. If he takes the Pawn, he gets a standard position (see p. 94) where the game is a draw. If he takes the Bishop — this is the natural reaction — he has another standard position. However, this one is a loss.

It is clear that the more end-game positions a player is able to recognize, the better are his chances of (a) winning his won games or (b) salvaging his lost ones.

Though, in the end-game, few pieces are left on the chessboard, there are many end-game positions. Thick books have been written about them.

You are not expected to know all of them. But you ought to know some of the more basic situations, which are draws, which are wins. And, if they are wins — how you should go about winning them.

It is very easy to win if one has a King and Queen against King. In the following position, the White King and Queen are as far apart as they could be. Yet, in a handful of moves, the Black King will be mated.

One must limit the enemy King's mobility and force him to a side of the board. Thus:

1	Q–K8	K–Q3
2	K–N2	

One must get one's King into action.

	. . .	K–Q4
3	K–B3	K–B4
4	Q–Q7	K–N3
5	K–N4	K–R3

The King has now been forced to the side of the chessboard. But at this point, one must be especially *careful not to allow a stalemate.* This would happen if White carelessly played Q–QB7, instead of

6	K–B5	K–R4

White now has a choice of mates. He can play his Queen to either N5 or R7!

In mating with a King and Rook, the principle is the same. You must limit the enemy King and force him to the edge of the chessboard. The procedure will take longer. Still it will not be too difficult.

In this position, if Black plays K–B3, White plays R–Q5. If Black plays K–B2, White plays R–K6. On K–Q2, White moves K–B5. *If White is on move,* he retreats his King to K4. Then, after Black's move, he resumes his driving tactics.

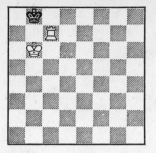

This is a typical mating position. If it is Black's move, his only choice is K–R1. Then R–B8 mates. If it's White's move, he retreats his Rook along the Bishop-file. Black again plays K–R1. White again mates on B8.

In the first diagram that we had on the preceding page, substitute a Rook for the Queen. (White: K at QR1. R at KR8. Black: K at Q4.)

The game might go as follows:

1 R–K8	K–Q3	10 R–Q6	K–N2
2 K–N2	K–Q2	11 K–Q5	K–B2
3 R–K4	K–Q3	12 K–B5	K–N2
4 K–B3	K–Q4	13 R–B6	K–R2
5 K–Q3	K–Q3	14 R–B7 ch	K–R1
6 K–B4	K–B3	15 K–N6	K–N1
7 R–K6 ch	K–B2	16 R–B1	K–R1
8 K–Q5	K–Q2	17 R–B8 *checkmate*	
9 K–K5	K–B2		

You follow the same procedure when you try to mate with 2 Bishops. The most important difference is that it is not enough to force the King to the side of the board. You must drive him *into the corner*.

This is the typical mate.

If we start with this position, the game might proceed as follows:

1 K–N7		K–Q4
2 K–B6		K–K5
3 B–B6 ch		K–Q5
4 B–B2 ch		K–B5
5 K–K5		K–Q6
6 B–N5 ch		K–B6
7 B–K1 ch		K–B7
8 K–Q4		K–Q8
9 B–N4		K–B7
10 B–R4 ch		K–B8
11 K–B3		K–N8
12 B–R3		K–R7
13 B–B1		K–N8
14 K–Q2		K–R7
15 K–B2		K–R8
16 B–N2 ch		K–R7
17 B–N3 mate		

This mate is much more difficult. But, as if to compensate, it is also much more rare. You would do well to practice it. Not because you'll need it — you may play 1000 games without your coming across it. But it will give you experience in coordinating the pieces.

This is also true of a mate with Knight and Bishop. In fact, it is even harder. As you recall, the weaker side can invoke the 50-move law. In your first attempts, you will probably take longer and the game will be a draw. When you gain precision, it will take you about 30.

Because it is so hard, it makes an excellent exercise. Try placing the pieces in different places on the board, then set yourself the problem of mating in fewer than 50 moves. This time you must drive the King into one of the two corners that is *controlled by the Bishop*. The King therefore tries to run into one of the other two corners. In the following diagram, White can only mate at KR1 and QR8.

The game might go as follows — (Each side could make different moves.   But the principle would be the same.)

1 N–N3 ch	K–Q4	17 N–K5	K–B1
2 B–B3 ch	K–Q3	18 N–Q7 ch	K–K1
3 K–N5	K–K3	19 K–K6	K–Q1
4 N–Q4 ch	K–K4	20 K–Q6	K–K1
5 K–B5	K–B3	21 B–N6ch	K–Q1
6 K–Q6	K–B2	22 B–R5	K–B1
7 N–B5	K–B3	23 N–B5	K–Q1
8 N–K7	K–N2	24 N–N7 ch	K–B1
9 K–K6	K–R2	25 K–B6	K–N1
10 K–B6	K–R3	26 K–N6	K–B1
11 N–B5 ch	K–R2	27 B–N4 ch	K–N1
12 B–K4	K–N1	28 B–K6	K–R1
13 N–Q6	K–R1	29 N–B5	K–N1
14 N–B7 ch	K–N1	30 N–R6 ch	K–R1
15 B–B5	K–B1	31 B–Q5 *mate*	
16 B–R7	K–K1		

 A

 B

One of the key endings is a King and Pawn against King.   Some of its variants are wins.   Others are no more than draws.   Thus:

In diagram A — if White is on move, the game is a draw.

White plays K–K6.   (Otherwise, he loses the Pawn.)   This leads to a stalemate!

If, however, Black is on move, it is an easy win for White.   Black plays K–B2.   White plays K–Q7.   On his next move — he queens!

In diagram B — if White is on move, he plays P–K7 ch.   Black plays K–K1.   We are back in diagram A.   The game is a draw.

If Black is on move — he plays K–K1.   White plays P–K7. This is diagram A.   It is an easy win for White!

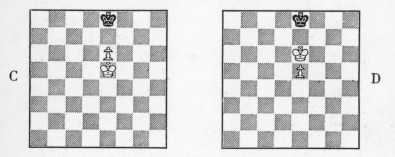

C   D

In general, the player with the Pawn tries to get his King in front of it.   He will win if he can do so.   If he cannot — he will *draw*.

Thus, diagram C is a draw *no matter who is on move*.   If White moves K–Q6, Black plays K–Q1.   We are back in diagram B.   If Black is on move, he plays K–K2!   In order to protect the Pawn, White plays K to Q5 or B5.   Black retreats to K1!!!

Diagram D, on the contrary, is a win *no matter who moves*.   If White is on move, he plays to Q6 (or B6).   Black moves to ·Q1 (or B1). White plays P–K6. He now has a winning form of diagram B. If Black is on move — if he plays K–Q1, White plays K–B7. If Black plays K–B1, White plays K–Q7. Either way, Black can't stop the Pawn from Queening. The game is a win!

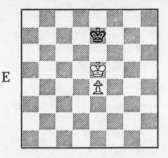

E

F

In diagram E, if Black is on move, White has a similar win. If Black moves K–Q2, White plays K–B6! If, however, White is on move, the game is only a draw. Thus, on K–Q5, Black plays K–Q2. On P–K5, Black plays K–K2. Then, on P–K6, Black plays K–K1. We are back in diagram C.

Diagram F is a win. If Black is on move, White follows the same procedure as he does in the previous diagram. If White is on move, he plays K–Q5 (or B5). Black plays K–Q2 (or B2). White plays P–K4! He now has a winning form of diagram E.

If the Pawn is a Rook Pawn, the *game is a draw.*

Here White cannot get the Black King away from R1. When the Pawn gets to R7, Black is stalemated.

The White King has to shuttle between R7 and R8. If he moves to a different square, the Black King gets to R1. When the Pawn gets to R7, a curious thing happens. The *Black King stalemates White.*

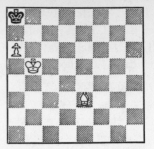

In this position, White also has a Knight, but the game is still a draw. (This is so only with the Pawn at R7.) Black shuttles between his R1 and N2. White cannot stop him unless he permits a stalemate.

White has a RP and Bishop. If the Bishop can't control the queening-square (R8), it does not matter where the Pawn is. The game is a draw. There is no way to evict the Black King from R1 without allowing a stalemate. (If White had his other Bishop instead of this one, it would be a simple win.)

In the next type of ending, when the two Kings face each other, with only a single square between them, the player who is *not* on move is said to *have the opposition*. In other parts of the game, it is good to be on move. It carries with it an initiative. But, in such an ending, it is always to one's advantage — though this may not be decisive — to have the opposition.

If we turn to p. 92, we see that, in Diagram D, Black's position is so bad that it does not matter which of the two players is on move. In B and E, however, the opposition is of more critical importance. If he *has* it, Black can *draw*. He *loses* if he *hasn't*.

In Diagram F, the White player has some leeway. If he hasn't the opposition, he can get it by moving his Pawn.

When the opposition is important, *it is always good to have one or two Pawn-moves to spare*.

When each side has Pawns, the opposition is equally important. Each player tries to get access to the other's Pawns. But, when the Kings face each other, the position is in a deadlock. The player who commits himself is at a disadvantage.

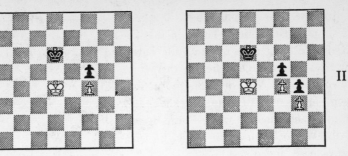

Diagram I: If White is on move, he plays K–B4. Black can't play K–K4. This being the case, the best he can do is to play K–B3, If, however, Black is on move, the White King wins the Pawn. *E.g.,* 1 . . . K–K3; 2 K–B5, K–K2; 3 K–Q5, K–B3; 4 K–Q6, K–B2; 5 K–K5, K–N3; 6 K–K6 . . . Then, after Black's next move, White captures the BP.

Yet, in this position, that is not enough to win! On 6 . . . K–N2, after White plays KxP, Black plays K–B2. *Black* has the *opposition.* It is a drawing variation of Diagram E.

In Diagram II, the first moves are the same. But, after taking the BP, White goes on to take the NP. After this, White wins easily.

Diagram III is like Diagrams I & II. But, in this position, since it is protected by the NP, White cannot win the BP. This game is a draw.

In Diagram IV — White wins if Black is on move. If Black plays K–B3, White plays K–K5. If Black moves K–K3, White plays K–B5. If, however, White is on move, he is able to draw by either K–B3 or K–K3. *K–Q3* is inferior. Black plays K–Q4! He has the opposition: and wins!

Another type of end-game is a matter of simple arithmetic. Thus, in this position, the King tries to catch the Pawn. He tries to get to QN2 before the White Pawn queens. We count the moves that each side needs. If the Black King is on move, he wins the race — and draws. If the White Pawn is on move, he wins the race — and wins.

A more frequent race is where two Pawns race to queen.

If the Pawns are equidistant from the 8th — or queening — rank, the game is almost always a draw. (All things being equal, it is clear that one player's K+Q is not in any way superior to the other's Q-K.) It may sometimes happen that the first player to queen does so with a check. The extra move he gains by this may give him a winning advantage.

Some of the other exceptions are seen in these diagrams:

Here the player who queens first controls the other's queening-square. He takes the other's Queen — and wins. Notice that if either King is placed on this long diagonal, the other queens with check — and wins.

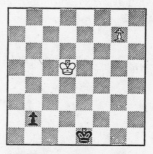

If White queens first, he *wins.* 1 P–N8(Q), P–N8(Q); 2 Q–N1 ch . . . if Black queens first, *he* wins. He checks on the diagonal and captures White's new Queen.

If White is on move, this game is a draw. If Black is on move, his best try is K–Q3. White plays K–B5. Each King captures a Pawn. Then, in the resulting Pawn-race, we get the following position. The White player is on move.

His winning procedure is as follows: a) he stops the Pawn from queening; b) he forces the other King in front of the Pawn; c) he brings his own King over.

1 Q–N3 ch	K–R7
2 Q–B2	K–N6
3 Q–K3 ch	K–B7
4 Q–K4 ch	K–B8
5 Q–B4 ch	K–Q7
6 Q–N3	K–B8
7 Q–B3 ch	K–N8

Now, in this position, with the Pawn blocked by his King, White can bring his own King nearer.

1 K–K3	K–R7
2 Q–B2	K–R8
3 Q–R4 ch	K–N8
4 K–Q3	

K–Q2 is a stalemate.

| | K–B8 |

5 Q–B2 mate!

If the Pawn has not reached the 7th rank, the Queen has an easy win. It does not matter where either of the Kings is located. If the Pawn is on the 7th, then the *file* becomes important. We just saw how the Queen wins if the Pawn is on the Knight-file. It wins in similar fashion, if it's on the King- or the Queen-file.   If it's on the Rook- or Bishop-file, the game is usually drawn.

The Queen cannot force the King in front of the Pawn. Here the King goes to R8. QxP creates a stalemate. If you try these, you will see that in neither of these diagrams does the White King get a chance to move nearer to the action.

Here the Queen does force the King in front of the Pawn. But, the moment that it does so, the Queen has to move itself in order to remove the stalemate.

If the Queen is able to get in front of the Pawn — or if the White King is near enough to the scene of the action, the game is a win. White plays Q–Q2 ch. Black must play K–N8. White

plays K–N4! Black moves P–R8 (Q). White plays K–N3!! Now, in the above position, Black — although he has a Queen — is not able to stop mate.

In the next diagram, Black's King has to stop White's QRP from queening. White's King has to stop Black's QBP. Thus, neither King can move over to the King-side Pawns before he has disposed of the opposing Pawn.

When White captures the BP and Black captures the RP the White

King will be 2 squares nearer to the group of Pawns on the King-side. It does not matter which of the two players is on move. Because of the Pawn-position, the White player will win. (Try this on your chess board!)

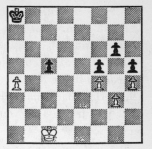

The QBP has no hostile Pawns in front of it. Neither are there hostile

Pawns in the files adjacent to it. In other words, no hostile Pawn can stop this Pawn from queening. Such a Pawn is known as a *passed pawn*. The QRP is a *passed pawn* likewise.

In such positions, the *outside passed pawn* wins!

In the above position, though either player is able to move his KNP, such a move would be disastrous. For all practical purposes, the King-side Pawns are locked. Neither side can make a break and establish a passed pawn.

There are positions, however, in which a break-through is possible. It might be wise to look at a number of pawn-positions and see whether or not a passed pawn can be established.

As a general thing, when two equal groups of pawns are opposed to one another, neither side can stage a break-through.

There is one exception:

A   B

In diagram *A*, with the Black player on move, Black can force a break-through by playing P–N6. If White plays RPxP, Black — (as in diagram *B*) — moves P–B6. If White plays BPxP, Black moves P–R6 and wins. If White plays P–R3, Black's Pawn takes the NP. In either of these variations, the Black Pawn is able to queen a number of moves before White does.

In diagram *A*, with the White player on move, he is able to forestall the break-through by his playing *P–N3*. White will lose if, instead of doing this, he chooses to move a Pawn to either B3 or R3. On P–B3, Black moves P–R6. On P–R3, Black moves P–B6.

If you try this on your chessboard, you will see that Black will win.

If the Pawns are not equal, the side having the majority can usually stage a break-through.

The above is the typical case. No matter what Black does, White is left with a passed pawn.

The Pawn on B3 — for rather obvious reasons — is called a *backward pawn*. The presence of a backward pawn may reduce the worth of one's majority. In this position, if White plays P–B4, Black will queen as soon as White does.

Here we have a special case. The 2 White Pawns are able to contain their 3 opponents.

If Black plays P–N3 — (on PxP, Black plays PxP and wins) — White plays P–N5! No matter what Black does, White gets a Queen on the Rook-file.

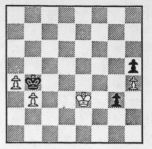

The Black King has to stay on the Queen-side; the White one on the King-side. If Black takes the Pawn on N3, he will not be able to stop the Pawn on R4 from queening. Though he has an extra Pawn, White is similarly handcuffed. This game is a draw.

Black's passed pawn on KN6 is no longer connected to his RP. White will take this Pawn and win. White's pawns are *connected*. As opposed to this, the Black pawns are *isolated*.
Isolated pawns are a weakness!

Here is an exception. If the White King moves to B4, Black plays P–R5. White cannot take the BP. If the White King moves to R4, Black plays P–B5. (The Black Pawns function just as if they were connected.)

The White Pawns lack the time to set up a like formation. Though White is on move, the Black King gets to KB3 before the White Pawn reaches R6.

A *double-pawn* — two pawns on the same file — are another form of weakness.

In this position, neither can protect the other. The White King can pick them off.

The White Pawn on KN4 can contain the *double-pawn.* Black has a King-side majority, but this majority is useless. If you try this on your chessboard, you will see that White will win.

From the very first moves — even while he thinks of mates or how to gain material — a player should be aware of the fact that the game may reach the end-game. If it does, his pawn-position may be the determining factor. Thirty or forty moves later, he may win because of a passed pawn or a pawn-majority that he has just established. He may lose because he has a backward, isolated or doubled pawn that, at the present time, seems to have no bearing on the game.

Pure Pawn endings — that is, those involving no more than a King and Pawns — are the easiest to win. If you have a material advantage, try to exchange your pieces. Try to hold on to your Pawns. And, conversely, if you have a material disadvantage, try to hold on to your pieces. Try to exchange your Pawns!

Endings that involve the other pieces are much more difficult. It is not feasible to give these a comprehensive treatment. (Thick books have been written on the subject.) In the next few pages, we will give some rules of thumb and show some of the key-positions.

A minor piece — a Bishop or a Knight — is usually able to draw against a minor piece and Pawn. The player with the single piece tries to give it up for the Pawn. When he succeeds, his opponent is a piece ahead. But, as we have seen, a single Bishop or Knight is not enough for a mate.

The above does not apply to a Rook + Pawn *vs.* Rook. It does not pay a player to give his Rook for the Pawn. The opponent still has a Rook. This is enough to force a checkmate.

If the other cannot get his King in front of the Pawn, the player with the Pawn should win. The key-position follows:

1 R–K1 ch	K–B2
2 R–K4!!	R–N8
3 K–Q7	R–Q8 ch
4 K–B6	R–B8 ch
5 K–N6	R–N8 ch
6 K–B5!	R–B8 ch
7 R–B4	

Black can't stop the Pawn from queening.

Notice the importance of 2 R–K4. This position comes up often. And in every case, the Rook must go to the 4th rank.

This is *the only winning procedure.*

If the other King is able to get in front of the Pawn, then the game is probably a draw.

In this diagram, it's a win if White is on move.

1 K–N6	R–Q1
2 R–N7 ch	K–R1
3 R–R7 ch	K–N1
4 P–B7 ch	K–B1
5 R–R8 ch	K–K2

Then, after the exchange of Rooks, P–B8 queens.

If Black is on move — he draws.

1 . . .		R–N8
2	K–N6	R–N8 ch
3	K–B5	K–B1
4	K–K6	R–K8 ch etc.

If Black plays with any care, he will *always* be on move when that position is reached.

If the Pawn is a RP, a win is especially difficult.

When there are Pawns on both sides of the board, a long-range piece like the Bishop is usually more effective than a Knight. This is especially true when the Pawn position is fluid. If the Pawn position is locked, the Knight will tend to be superior.

It is a good rule not to place one's Pawns on the same color as one's Bishop. These impair the Bishop's value. In such positions, the Knight is also superior.

In Pawn+Bishop endings, if the opposing Bishops stand on squares of opposite colors, the result is frequently a draw — even if one player has 1 or 2 Pawns more than the other.

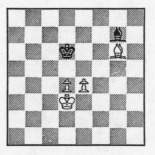

Thus, in this position, the White Pawns can make no progress. After P–Q5, the Black King is impregnable. On P–K5 ch, Black plays BxP. This game is a draw!

K+Q should win against a K+R. K+R should draw against K+R+B. However, this is both lengthy and difficult. In the hands of an inexperienced player, this last ending frequently is lost.

Before we leave the ending, let us look at one last finale and notice how many fertile ideas there may occasionally be in one apparently simple position. Since a King + Queen will win against a King + Rook, Black tries to exchange his Rook for the White Pawn. If he can, the game is a draw. White, of course tries to prevent this. If he can, the game is won.

In this position, if Black were only on move, there would not be any problem. R-Q3 pins the Pawn. And, on his next move, Black plays *RxP* and *draws*.

However, White is on move! He plays P-B7. Now the Black Rook has no pin. In addition, the Pawn is threatening to Queen on the very next move. Black still plays R-Q3. This time, it's with *check!*

If White plays K-N7, Black R-Q2 — draw. If White plays to the Rook-file, R-B3 — draw. If White plays K-B5, Black plays R-Q8. If White follows this by queening, Black plays R-B8 check — and actually wins. White must play K-N5. Black plays R-Q4 check. In this fashion, the two pieces move on their respective files — until R-Q6 check. Then White moves K-B2. (See diagram above.)

Now Black is in trouble. R-Q8 will be answered by the simple KxR. Black can't stop the Pawn from queening. But Black still has a trick! He plays R-Q5. On P-B8(Q), R-B5 ch. White plays QxR and — it is a stalemate!

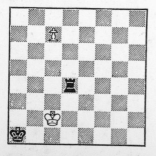

The White player sees this danger. He avoids it by under-promotion. P–B8 (R)! The game is even. Each side has a K+R. And, almost always, such a game would be a draw. But, in this position, White is threatening mate by R–R8 ch.

Black can't stop this threat. He plays R–QR5.

White now plays K–N3. This gives him a double *attack*. He threatens KxR as well R–B1 mate. Black cannot stop both threats.

After all of these thrusts and counter-thrusts, White finally has a win.

Hints for the Opening and Middle-Game

In the end-game, the beginner has the same problems as the expert. If a move is good for one, it is also good for the other. This is not the case in *the opening*. The beginner and the expert do have the same objectives. They try to mobilize their pieces: to bring them to emplacements where they have a maximum potential. And, in order to achieve this, chess theorists have developed a number of *general principles*.

These are not rigid. The expert does not follow them blindly. He feels free to depart from them whenever he thinks it advantageous. The learner, on the other hand, would do well to follow them closely. In time, he will break these also. But, before he does so, he should learn what rules he is violating.

If you're White, *play P–K4*. This is not a rule. But, when playing King-Pawn openings, it is easier to learn the basic rules and ideas. For similar reasons — if you're Black, and White plays P–K4, you should *answer P–K4*.

In the early part of the game, keep the major pieces out of action. If you move them you expose them and you enable your opponent to *gain many moves in his development!*

Here Black gains a move by playing *N–KB3*. On 1 QxNP, Black plays R–N1; 2 Q–R6, BxP ch. (If 3 KxB, N–N5 ch.) 3 K–Q1, R–N3; 4 Q–R3, P–Q4. By attacking the Queen, Black has been developing his pieces. After 5 Q–Q3, he can win in several ways. For example, 5 . . . BxN, followed by 6 . . . P–Q5 and 7 . . . N–N5.

It is even more important to keep the King out of action. In the latter parts of the game — especially when Queens are gone — the King will do his share. In the early parts, the essential thing *is safety*. Except for castling, *you should 'not move your King*.

In the first 10-12 moves, *the only Pawns that you should play are the King-Pawn and the Queen-Pawn*. For the inexperienced player, *it is* particularly *dangerous to advance the King-Bishop-Pawn*.

The first diagram shows you the *earliest possible checkmate*. For very obvious reasons, this mate is called the *Fool's Mate*. There is no good reason why White should have made these moves. Still this diagram shows you the danger of weak Pawn-moves.

In the second diagram, Black's move is a bit more plausible. The BP defends the KP. Yet, because he moved his BP, his position is inferior. White plays NxP. After PxN, Q–R5 ch. Then, after P–N3, QxKP ch.

Do not block your pieces.

Move your Knights before your Bishops. The Knights are best at KB3 or QB3. The King-Bishop should move to either B4 or N5. If you are Black, it can also go to K2. The Queen-Bishop should move to K3 or N5.

Try to centralize your pieces. Also, try to keep a *Pawn at K4 or at Q4*.

Do not move the same piece twice. Don't exchange a piece that you have developed for a piece your rival hasn't. As a matter of fact, do not exchange any pieces unless you have a good reason.

This applies to Pawns as well. Do not move one more than once. Get your King-Pawn to the 4th rank, your Queen-Pawn to the 3rd or 4th. If you move them to the 5th rank, this may prove a weakness later.

Castle early — preferably on the King-side. Don't attack too soon. (If you are Black, this rule is especially important.) Yet, your moves ought to be *aggressive*. A Knight at KB3 attacks the Pawn at K5. A Bishop at QB4 attacks the Pawn at KB7. These points may be well protected, but if you apply the pressure, your rival must continue to defend them! And if he slips (see p. 55), you are ready to demolish him!

These rules are in the nature of *Do not cross the street* or *Don't go near the fire!* Children see their elders do so. But, before they know when it is perfectly safe, they had best not do it themselves! The same applies to chess. If you watch the games of experts, you will see that these rules are continually being violated. It's another case of *Do what I say. Do not do what I do!*

Let there be a reason for every move. What is more — do not think of single moves! You should think in terms of a sequence, of a *plan*.

Remember that a move is not good or bad *per se*. It is good or it is bad in a *particular position*. Build your plans around what is happening in that position!

A chess game is a war, a *contest*. You must *consider your opponent*. He is more or less your equal. (It is not good to play a player who is much stronger or much weaker than you are.) If you are making plans, your opponent is doing the same.

Being human, he is sure to make some errors. If you win, it will be because he makes them. You must therefore be alert to take advantage of·such errors. But, when he seems to blunder, you should first make sure that it isn't part of a trap. When he makes a move, try to put yourself in his place. Determine what *he is up to*.

When you make attacks or threats, he will probably see them. Think in terms of his answer. Where will your pieces and Pawns be? *Who will have a better position after he has countered your threats?*

If you have a *better position*, you should try to turn this into a more tangible advantage. How to do this is a thing that can't be taught. Perhaps you should concentrate your pieces on an opposing weak point. Or perhaps you should make a *double attack*. But, although you can learn the end-game and, to a lesser degree, how to find your way through the opening, there is no one who can show you how to devise a maneuver or combination that is both ingenious and accurate. That can come only with experience.

When he first begins to play, it is only natural that a student should feel uncertain. But, after a while — like a child learning to walk — the beginner gets some confidence. In fact, he gets over-confident and goes in for a period of rather reckless experimentation.

This is all for the best. No matter how much inborn talent a beginner may have, he must play a lot of games before he starts to really get *the feel of the pieces*. He will benefit greatly if these games are tense, if they're full of tricks and traps, of successful — and unsuccessful — combinations and sacrifices, stratagems and maneuvers.

Prudence is the watch-word. But, after you have learned to thread your way through the opening, it would be well if you followed your inclinations, if you made a reversal and suddenly began to play in a more audacious fashion.

This is the type of game to which you will be attracted — the kind you will try to emulate.

This type of chess may be exemplified in the diagram that follows:

On the 23rd move — (this was played in Breslau, 1912) — Frank J. Marshall, Black, who was playing S. Lewitzky, moved his Queen from QB6 to KN6, giving rise to this position.

Note that the Black Queen now can be taken in *3* different ways. If RPxQ, Black plays N–K7 *mate*. On BPxQ, N–K7 ch. Then, when White plays K–R1, Black plays RxR *mate*.

White's best move is QxQ. Black plays N–K7 ch. After K–R1, Black plays NxQ ch. White cannot retake the Knight. Then, after K–N1, NxR; PxR . . . Black has a prosaic but very simple win!

Marshall was showered with gold pieces for this victory.

Then, in time, you will begin to see that there are other methods which are equally effective. In this position — (1923, Copenhagen) — A. Nimzovich was Black. F. Saemisch was White. On his 25th move, Black played P–KR3.

Now look at this diagram. White is ahead in material. To be precise, he has a piece for 2 Pawns. Yet he is completely helpless.

If he moves the Knight, it is taken by the Pawn. If his QB moves to B1, the Black Bishop takes the Knight. If the Rook at K1 moves, Black plays R–K7 and the White Queen is trapped. If White plays the Rook at N1, Black plays BxR. If B–KB1, Black plays BxB. The White Queen has no move which will not result in capture. If White goes K–R2, the King-Bishop is pinned. Black plays R(4)–B6. The White Queen has no move. *Black's last move — P–KR3 — has removed White's last escape-square.*

At this point, White resigned!

This type of chess will not completely replace the slashing attacks of an Anderssen or Morphy. But, when you begin to use it, you will have another useful weapon in your repertory.

This new tool may be more quiet. Yet, in its way, it is equally spectacular!

In 1858, the young American genius, Morphy, played the following game in Paris against the Duke of Brunswick, who was playing in consultation with Count Isuard. (Incidentally, this was played at the opera during a performance of Rossini's *Barber of Seville*.)

Paul Morphy	Allies
1 P–K4	P–K4
2 N–KB3	P–Q3
3 P–Q4	B–N5?
4 PxP	BxN

On 4 . . . PxP; 5 QxQ ch, KxQ; 6 NxP.

        5 QxB   PxP
        6 B–QB4   N–KB3
        7 Q–QN3

A double attack.

        7 . . . .   Q–K2
        8 N–B3

Rather than take the NP, White plays for bigger game. On 8 QxNP, Black plays Q–N5 ch, forcing an exchange of Queens.

        8 . . . .   P–B3
        9 B–KN5   P–N4
       10 NxP   PxN
       11 BxNP ch   QN–Q2
       12 O–O–O!   R–Q1

This protects the Knight. But — it's not enough.

       13 RxN   RxR
       14 R–Q1   Q–K3

The Black Knight is no longer pinned. On 15 BxR ch, Black can now play NxB.

Sure enough!

       15 BxR ch   NxB

Black is now a piece ahead. Yet, oddly enough, this is the precise position that White has been playing for.

       16 Q–N8 ch   . . . .

       (See the Diagram.)

       16 . . . .   NxQ

Black can make no other move!

17 R–Q8 checkmate.

After only 16 moves, the only pieces White has left are a Bishop and a Rook. However, these 2 pieces are enough to force a mate!

In this game, the noble lords did not offer much opposition. In a sense, Morphy was shooting fish in a barrel. In the game that follows, the loser also contributed his share of the pyrotechnics.

A. Anderssen	L. Kieseritzky
1 P–K4	P–K4
2 P–KB4	PxP
3 B–B4	P–QN4
4 BxP	Q–R5 ch
5 K–B1	N–KB3
6 N–KB3	Q–R3
7 P–Q3	N–R4

His threat is N–N6 ch.

8 N–R4	P–QB3
9 N–B5	Q–N4
10 P–KN4	N–B3

Now, if White protects the NP, Black will take the Bishop, and if White protects the Bishop, Black will capture the NP.

White prefers to do the former. But he has a reason.

11 R–N1	PxB
12 P–KR4	Q–N3
13 P–R5	Q–N4
14 Q–B3	N–N1

He must make an escape-square for his Queen.

15 BxP	Q–B3
16 N–B3	B–B4
17 N–Q5	QxP
18 B–Q6	. . . .

(See the adjoining diagram.)

18 . . . .   BxR
19 P–K5   . . . .

This shuts off the Queen from the Black Pawn on N2. White now threatens NxP ch — followed by B–B7 mate!

19 . . . .   QxR ch
20 K–K2   N–QR3

Stopping NxP ch, followed by B–B7 mate.

21 NxP ch   K–Q1

(See adjoining diagram.) By this time, White has sacrificed 2 Rooks as well as a Bishop.

22 Q–B6 ch   . . . .

Now White gives up even more — this the biggest piece of all. The Black move is forced.

22 . . . .   NxQ

Now — at last —

23 B–K7 checkmate.

White has given up a Queen, a Bishop and 2 Rooks. In return for this, he has just a single Pawn. Oh, yes! And a brilliant checkmate.

This was played in London in 1851. Since then it is known as *The Immortal Game.*

LESSONS IN STRATEGY AND TACTICS *Illustrated*

Chess, like love, like music, according to Grandmaster Dr. Siegbert Tarrasch, has the power to make men happy. Before you are able to participate in this genial adventure, however, chess must become a part of you, a sort of second nature. You must learn to play with ease and abandon.

On the following pages are two practice games. They are each short, smart and sweet. Curiously, despite their brevity, they were played by masters. They are presented by photographs and diagrams so that you will be guided in the correct execution of the moves. Play them over and over again until you are able to make each move without a moment's hesitation.

At first, you may find the Knight moves a bit troublesome. After a while, as you perceive the irregular movement of the Knight as a straight line, the play will become facile.

When you have mastered the mechanical movements of the men, you will give closer attention to the meaning of the moves. Then you will be in position to absorb strategy and tactics.

White's First Move　　　1 P–Q4　　....

There are many ways in which to begin a chess game. Nowadays, the two most favored openings start with the advance of the King Pawn two squares or with the advance of the Queen Pawn two squares. Each of these moves leads to a different and distinct pattern.

The advance of the Queen Pawn two squares is White's choice. This opening is called the Queen Pawn Game. In moving the Queen Pawn two squares, White is freeing his Queen Bishop and his Queen for future action. He is also attempting to control some squares in the center of the board, which his Pawn at Q4 now attacks. These are his K5 and QB5, the latter being near the center.

Black's First Move   1 . . . .   N–KB3

Black, too, has a wide choice in his reply on the first move. Legally, it is possible to make any one of twenty different moves. Each of the eight Pawns can move either one or two squares, for a total of sixteen moves, and each Knight can move two squares, making a grand total of twenty.

Black's choice is to bring out his King Knight. He may have several reasons for doing so. Theoretically, his reason is to control central squares with his Knight — his Q4 and K5. Practically, he may select this defense because he may think he knows a little more about it than his opponent. Or he may try to steer the ensuing play in a trappy line. Setting traps in the opening is usually not good strategy. But it works here.

White's Second Move   2 N–Q2   . . . .

Again, White has a wide choice of moves. The one he selects is playable, but it is not the best. A better move, for example, is to bring out the King Knight to KB3. At B3 the Knight controls more important squares in the center. The text move blocks the Queen Bishop.

It is important, of course, to bring out a piece at each turn in the opening. Here, White is following that precept. It is equally important, however, to place that piece on a square which enjoys good present and future prospects. White's move is deficient in that respect. The Knight in the center of the board (at B3) enjoys greater prospects. It does not, moreover, interfere with the mobility of the Bishop when at B3.

Black's Second Move   2 . . . .   P–K4

Black's move must be viewed with suspicion. He is offering a Pawn, apparently for no reason at all. To take it or not to take it will be White's problem. For the moment, Black's play must be considered as courageous or cunning or stupid. For a Pawn is a very valuable unit.

Because White's last move was not quite orthodox and creates a possible setting for a trap, Black gambles a Pawn. This is a calculated risk. If the Pawn is not captured, Black will have no qualms. If the Pawn is captured, Black will attempt to retrieve it, while at the same time creating a snare for his (he hopes) unsuspecting adversary. A calculated risk is not always good strategy. At times, it wins games.

White's Third Move   3 PxP   . . . .

White captures Black's Pawn. Is this procedure good, bad or indifferent? There is a facetious maxim in chess: "Take first and look later." Is that the case here? Or is White making the capture out of sound conviction? The following moves may tell the story.

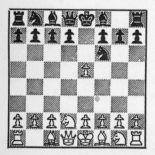

To take or not to take is a problem which confounds beginner and expert alike. There are, of course, times when an offering should be accepted, and other times when it should be declined. Unfortunately, there is no general principle which supplies the answer. To take the offering when you see no good reason for declining is sound practice. If it should develop that there was a good reason which you did not see, then you will have been richly rewarded in experience.

Black's Third Move   3 . . . .   N–N5

Because Black's Knight is now attacked by White's King Pawn, Black moves his Knight. He moves it to a square, however, from which he menaces White's King Pawn and threatens to retrieve it. Innocent as it seems, Black's move is brimful of danger.

Black's last move is all part and parcel of a deep laid plan. At worst, Black hopes to recover his Pawn. At best, he hopes for bigger things . . . But we are getting ahead of our story. There are various ways in which White can now defend his Pawn. But Black can attack the King Pawn with more force than White can defend it. Clearly, Black's calculated risk has not been badly calculated. He is now ready to pile on to the King Pawn.

White's Fourth Move   4 P–KR3?   . . . .

White sees that he cannot safely defend the King Pawn. For example, if he played 4 N–KB3, Black would play N–QB3 and eventually, Black would pick off the Pawn. Hence, White decides to drive the Black Knight from its advanced post.

White's last move, as will be seen above, gets a question mark for a good and sufficient reason. Despite the fact that he cannot retain the extra King Pawn, he ought to continue to bring out his pieces. He is so obsessed, however, with the Black Knight lurking in his territory, he violates general principles. White's last Pawn move creates a most unusual situation. And Black is quick to profit.

Black's Fourth Move   4 . . . .   N–K6!

Black moves his Knight to K6. This move takes White completely by surprise. Clearly, White had counted upon Black playing NxKP. All of Black's earlier moves had pointed to that. The sudden change has caught White off balance.

Black's last move gets an exclamation point, despite the fact that Black is offering a Knight. Why? Because in chess parlance, it is a sockdolager. If White fails to take the Knight, the Knight will capture White's Queen. If White captures the Knight with 5 PxN, Black checkmates in two. 5 . . . Q–R5 check 6 P–KN3, QxP mate. The prospects of playing with a Queen down are so slim, White resigns. The game was actually played between Gibaud and Lazard in 1924.

White's First Move   1 P–K4   . . . .

In this game, White begins by advancing his King Pawn two squares. By doing so, he frees his King Bishop and Queen for future action. At the same time his Pawn at K4 controls the important square in the center, Q5, and the square near the center, KB5.

For a good many years the masters have argued about the relative strength of 1 P–K4 as against 1 P–Q4. There are those who have a predilection for one and there are those who favor the other. Each of these moves leads to a distinct pattern. The Queen Pawn game is usually less exciting in the beginning. The King Pawn game leads to more frills and thrills.

Black's First Move   1 . . . .   P–Q3

Black ought to advance his Pawn to K4, too. But he prefers to play it "safe." His first move is irregular. From a theoretical point of view, it is not so good, even though it does free the Queen Bishop for future action.

Observe that White's move controls important squares in Black's territory — White's Q5 and White's KB5. Observe that Black's move strikes only at squares on the fourth rank (from Black's side of the board). In evaluating these moves, it is clear, the difference is slight. One little advantage in chess does not mean much. The sum total of many small advantages, however, adds up.

White's Second Move   2 B–B4   . . . .

White makes immediate use of his King Bishop, which he freed on his first move. His move is an aggressive one. For the Bishop is directing its attack against the most vulnerable square in Black's camp, Black's KB2. This spells danger.

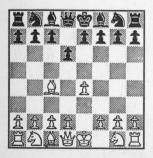

It is interesting to observe how the movement of one piece flows from the movement of another, in a properly co-ordinated game. Here, White's first move prepared for his second. And his second move is looking forward to future possibilities. Of course, Black is, or should be, aware of what White has in mind. And Black has adequate time and resource to take care of any brewing threats.

Black's Second Move   2 . . . .   N–Q2

Black brings out his Queen Knight to Q2. In doing so, he is following the general principle of development. He is bringing out his force to join the fray. There is, however, a drawback to Black's move. His Knight is interfering with the mobility of his Bishop.

A jester once remarked,"If you bring out your pieces, you are apt to lose them. If you do not bring them out, you are apt to lose because you do not bring them out." Black here is choosing the middle of the road. His Knight is out, yet close to home. The Knight, as has already been observed, is better posted on B3. From that square it controls more important squares.

White's Third Move   3 N–KB3   . . . .

White is playing straightforward chess. He posts his Knight on an excellent square from where it strikes important squares in the center of the board. Because Black has made slightly inferior moves, it does not follow that Black can be overwhelmed immediately.

Thus far, White has made three moves. Each move is good in that each move brings another piece into action, and each move has some bearing on the central squares. Because Black has played a backward game, White enjoys a freer position, a slight initiative. To convert such a small advantage into a win, however, is an exceedingly difficult process.

Black's Third Move   3 . . . .   P–KN3

Black has just advanced his King Knight Pawn to the third rank. This move is a prelude to bringing out the King Bishop to KN2. Black's plan is to develop the Bishop on the flank. Technically, in chess parlance, it is called fianchettoing the Bishop.

Black is choosing a round-about method of development. He is moving Pawns when he ought to be moving pieces. Usually, it is possible to make one or two inferior moves in the opening without suffering immediate loss. Here, however, the position is exceptional. White's men are all posted to advantage to institute a crushing combination. It is pretty and deep.

White's Fourth Move   4 BxP ch   . . . .

On his fourth move, White makes a startling sacrifice of material. He gives up a Bishop for a Pawn by playing 4 BxPch. There is more to this move than is apparent at first sight. White is looking a number of moves ahead into the future.

Because Black has been remiss in his development and, particularly, because he has failed to guard his vulnerable point, his KB2, White inaugurates a powerful attack beginning with a violent sacrifice of a piece. There are no two ways about this move. Black must accept. Hence, the idea which White has in mind must be correct, or else. . . . .

Black's Fourth Move   4 . . . .   KxB

Black captures the White Bishop.   He does so because he has no choice.   He must now abide by whatever is in store for him.   He can only hope (and pray) that White has made a miscalculation. No longer is he able to steer the game as he chooses.

Black's lackadaisical development meets with hasty and just retribution. All of White's men happen to be on the correct squares for what is to follow. And, sadly, all of Black's men are poorly enough posted so as to make White's combination sound.   The King is going for a "ride" in a one-way traffic lane. There is, unfortunately, no return.

White's Fifth Move   5 N–N5 ch . . . .

By playing 5 N–N5, White checks the enemy King. White has visualized the ensuing variations and, if he is correct, he hopes to recover more material than he has given up. He must, of course, be correct. Otherwise he will be minus more material than he can afford.

The Knight check is only one of the tactical plays in a grand combination which White has made. The Bishop sacrifice was the first play. There are still several plays before the game reaches a conclusion. Thinking ahead is one of the attributes of a good chess-player. The ability to think ahead comes with over-the-board experience.

Black's Fifth Move   5 . . . .   K–B3

Black has moved his King to B3, attacking the White Knight. Here, Black had a choice of two other moves. He could see, however, that they would lose his Queen immediately. That is why he chose the text move. Black is still hoping that White will go astray.

Instead of the text move, Black might have returned his King to K1. In that case, however, White would play 6 N–K6. The Knight would attack and win Black's Queen. Or Black might have played his King to N2. In that case, White would continue with 6 N–K6ch, forking the Black King and Queen. Because of these possibilities, Black plays the text.

White's Sixth Move   6 Q–B3 ch   . . . .

White has just brought out his Queen to KB3, again checking the Black King. This move, too, is part and parcel of the grand combination which White began some time ago, by sacrificing his Bishop. White must continue his attack incessantly.

White's Queen check gives Black no rest. For Black is again obliged to move his King. Even though Black has three possible King moves at this turn, White is prepared for each one of them. Thus, from the first sacrifice to the present one (. . . KxN is possible), White is treading on tenuous ground.

Black's Sixth Move   6 . . . .   KxN

Black captures White's Knight. Of the three alternative lines, Black decides to take more material. Curiously, each of the other possibilities leads to a checkmate in two moves! Thus, 6 . . . K–N2 7 N–K6 ch, K–R3 8 Q–R3 mate, or 6 . . . K–K4 7 P–Q4 ch, KxP 8 Q–B3 mate.

Black captures White's Knight because if White has miscalculated, Black will be two pieces to the good. The onus of proving a checkmate now is upon White. And the checkmate, if there is one, is well concealed. For, as a general rule, it is difficult to mate an enemy King in the middle of the board with a lone Queen.

White's Seventh Move   7 P–Q4 dis ch

White's seventh move is an unusual one.   It is the advance of his Queen Pawn to the fourth rank, discovering a check by his Queen Bishop.   In this way, White is able to bring an additional attacking force to the sector of the adverse King.

The outcome of this game no longer hinges on small theoretical advantages. White has given up two pieces and he must quickly capitalize on his position. Black's King is the target.   Every move must be well directed, and White has no time to spare.   Uncovering the concealed Bishop is the hidden resource, and the attack continues unabated.

Black's Seventh Move   7 . . . .   K–R5

Black makes the only move available to him. He must escape the check. He is now completely at the mercy of his opponent, even though he is rich in material. Not a single Black man is able to assist in the defense.

The enforced march of the King has brought the monarch a long way from his throne. It is important to remember that every solemn step of the way can be attributed to the slightly inferior opening moves. Black should have brought out his pieces. He didn't. Now, unwillingly, he brings out his King to take the flailing enemy blows.

White's Eighth Move   8 Q–R3 checkmate

White plays his Queen to KR3 checkmate.   What a picture!   The Black King is attacked by the adverse Queen and there is no escape. All the squares surrounding the King are covered by White forces, and not a single Black unit can help.

The game is over.   The King is dead. Long live the King.